Talking Heads

Alan Bennett

BBC BOOKS

Published by BBC Books
A division of BBC Enterprises Ltd
Woodlands, 80 Wood Lane, London W12 0TT

First published 1988
Reprinted 1988 (seven times)
Reprinted 1989 (four times)
Reprinted 1990 (twice)

© Forelake Ltd 1988

ISBN 0 563 206225

Set by Phoenix Photosetting, Chatham, Kent
Printed and bound in Great Britian by
Redwood Press Limited, Melksham, Wiltshire

Contents

Introduction

These six monologues were written and recorded for BBC television in
1987. Forms, one is often led to think, dictate themselves, the material
demanding to be written in a particular way and no other. I would be
happy to think this were so with these pieces but I'm not sure it's true.
A Chip in the Sugar, for instance, or *Bed Among the Lentils* could both
have been written as plays proper. It would be fun to see Mr Turnbull,
Mrs Whittaker's fancy man, in the flesh (and his three-quarter-length
windcheater), or Mrs Shrubsole doing her ruthless flower arranging – see
them for ourselves, that is, rather than through the eyes of Graham and
Susan who narrate those respective stories. But then they would be
different stories, more objective, rounded and altogether fairer to the
people the narrator is talking about. None of these narrators after all is
telling the whole story. Geoffrey, Susan's husband, may be a nicer, more
forbearing man than her account of him might lead us to suppose, and Mr
Turnbull may not be quite the common fellow ('could have been a
bookie') the jealous Graham is so ready to disparage. And were these
monologues plays there would be room for qualification and extenuation,
allowances could be made, redemptions hinted at, a different point of
view. Instead there is a single point of view, that of the speaker alone with
the camera, and with the rest of the story pictured and peopled by the
viewer more effort is demanded of the imagination. In this sense to watch
a monologue on the screen is closer to reading a short story than watching
a play.

Admittedly it is a stripped-down version of a short story, the style of its
telling necessarily austere. 'Said' or 'says' is generally all that is required
to introduce reported speech, because whereas the novelist or short story
writer has a battery of expressions to choose from ('exclaimed', 'retorted',
'groaned', 'lisped'), in live narration such terms seem literary and
self-conscious. Adverbs too ('she remarked, tersely') seem to over-egg the
pudding or else acquire undue weight in the mouth of a supposedly artless
narrator. And these narrators are artless. They don't quite know what
they are saying and are telling a story to the meaning of which they are not
entirely privy. In *A Chip in the Sugar* Graham would not accept that he is
married to his mother, or Miss Ruddock in *A Lady of Letters* that she is
not a public-spirited guardian of morals. In *Soldiering On* Muriel ends up
knowing her husband ruined her daughter but is no closer to realising that

she had a hand in it too. Lesley in *Her Big Chance* thinks she has a great
deal to offer both as an actress and a person, and Susan, the vicar's wife in
Bed Among the Lentils, doesn't realise it's not just the woman in the
off-licence but the whole parish that knows she's on the drink. Only
Doris, the old lady who has fallen and broken her hip in *A Cream Cracker
Under the Settee*, knows the score and that she is done for, but though she
can see it's her determination to dust that's brought about her downfall,
what she doesn't see is that it's the same obsession that tidied her husband
into the grave.

I am disturbed as I was with a previous collection of television plays to
note so many repetitions and recurrences. There are droves of voluntary
workers, umpteen officials from the social services, and should there be a
knock on the door it's most likely to be a bearded vicar. Even Emily
Brontë turns up twice. If I'm guilty of repeating myself, on another count
I plead innocence. The suspicion of child abuse in *A Lady of Letters* and
the hint of it in *Soldiering On* might suggest I am straining after topicality.
My instinct is generally to take flight in the opposite direction and in fact
both these pieces were written and recorded before the subject began
regularly to hit the headlines, which it may well have ceased to do by the
time the programmes are transmitted. Since several of the characters fare
badly at the hands of social and community workers I might seem to be
taking a currently fashionable line here also. In the popular press
nowadays social workers are generally (and easily) abused. I have little
experience of them and to seem to line up with the *Sun* or the *Daily
Express* would dismay me. My quarrel with social work is not with its
praiseworthy practicalities but with the jargon in which it's sometimes
conducted. Graham's 'I am not being defensive about sexual intercourse;
she is my mother' is a protest about language.

Some of the events in these stories stem from actual occurrences in my
life, though they are often joined to it by a very narrow isthmus. The
funeral with which *Soldiering On* begins (though none of the characters in
it) was suggested by the funeral of the composer George Fenton's father,
who had been in Colditz and like Ralph had touched life at many points.
Though much of the church stuff in *Bed Among the Lentils* (including Mr
Medlicott the verger) comes from my childhood, the disaffection of Susan,
the vicar's wife, I can trace to opening a hymn book in the chapel of
Giggleswick School and finding in tiny, timid letters on the fly leaf, 'Get
lost, Jesus'. Of these six characters only Lesley, the small-part actress, is

wholly modern (while being quite old-fashioned). She and dozens like her
have auditioned for films and plays I've done in the last twenty years. One
of the first Lesley-like characters was a boy who came up for a part in
Forty Years On. The director asked him what he had done:

'I was in George Bernard Shaw.'

'What did you play?'

'The drums.'

Perky, undefeated, their hopes of stardom long since gone, these actors
retail the films and plays one might have glimpsed them in, playing
waiters or barmen or, like Lesley, travelling on the back of a farm cart
next to the star, wearing a shawl, the shawl 'original nineteenth-century
embroidery, all hand done'. I saw an actor for a part not long ago who had
been in a few episodes of *Emmerdale Farm*. 'I played the postman,' he said,
'only I haven't done any since. They don't seem to be getting much mail.'

Another obsession goes back to childhood. The dog dirt outside
Buckingham Palace that spoils Miss Ruddock's Awayday and the 'little
hairs all up and down' that rule out a dog for Doris betray a prejudice
inherited from my father, who was a butcher in Leeds. He was plagued by
dogs: 'Get out, you nasty lamppost-smelling little article,' he shouted once
as he raced some unfortunate mongrel from the shop, and now thirty years
later Doris has the line. It was my father too who had a craze for
fretwork, but whereas for Doris's husband Wilfred fretwork is just one of
his dreams ('toys and forts and whatnot, no end of money he was going to
make'), with Dad it was no dream. Sitting at his little treadle saw with
plans from *Hobbies Magazine* beside him he made forts and farms for my
brother and me, a toy butcher's shop once and wonderfully elaborate
constructions of ramps and trapdoors into which we shot marbles. This
was at the start of the Second War when toys were scarce, and for a few
years he was able to make a little money selling some of his stuff to a
toyshop down County Arcade off Briggate. It wasn't much though. 'You
want to ask a bit more,' my mam used to say. 'They take advantage of
you. That's your trouble, Walt, you won't push yourself.' Which sounds
like Doris again. Toy penguins were Dad's speciality, made out of three-
ply and set on a sturdy green four-wheeled cart. Did we ever come across
a child pulling one of these creations it was a big event and we would trail
behind, scanning the face of its small owner for any evidence of pleasure
in this (to me very dull) toy, Dad presumably experiencing some of the
same pleasure a writer gets when he catches someone reading his book.

It's with mixed feelings that I see tattoos are (twice) sniffed at, along with red paint, yellow gloves and two-tone cardigans. These disparagements too date back to home and childhood, where they were items in a catalogue of disapproval that ranged through (fake) leopardskin coats, dyed (blonde) hair to slacks, cocktail cabinets and statuettes of ladies with alsatian dogs on leash. In our house and in my mother's idiosyncratic scheme of things they were all common. Common is not an easy term to define without seeming to brand the user as snobbish or socially pretentious, which my mother wasn't. But it was always her distinction: I never remember my father making it, and both in its use and application common tended to be a woman's term. 'She's a common woman' one heard more often (was more common) than 'He's a common feller', perhaps because in those days women had more time and inclination to make such distinctions. A common woman was likely to swear or drink (or drink 'shorts'), to get all dolled up and go out leaving the house upside down and make no bones about having affairs. Enjoy herself, possibly, and that was the trouble; a common woman sidestepped her share of the proper suffering of her sex. What was also being criticised was an element of pretension and display (the dyed blonde hair, the too-tight slip-over, the face plastered with make-up). Elsie Tanner was a common woman, as with her curlers and too ready opinions is Hilda Ogden. And so, I thought as a child, was Mary Magdalen.

Sudden money augmented the risk and pools winners would find it hard to avoid the epithet. Hence the unfortunate tale of Vivien Nicholson, the Yorkshire pools winner and heroine of Jack Rosenthal's *Spend, Spend, Spend*. Her persistent car crashes and the dramas and notorieties of her personal life were never out of the *Evening Post*. 'Well,' my mother used to say, as Mrs N wrote off yet another of her cars and her lovers in some frightful motorway pile-up, 'she's a common woman.' No other explanation was necessary.

Places could be common too, particularly at the seaside. Blackpool was common (people enjoying themselves), Morecambe less so (not enjoying themselves as much), and Grange or Lytham not common at all (enjoyment not really on the agenda). If we ever did get to Blackpool we stayed at Cleveleys or Bispham, the refined end. To my brother and me (and I suspect to the local estate agents) refined just meant furthest away from the funfair. Not that where we stayed made much difference to the type of boarding house or the mixed bag we found there. To some extent my mother's nice distinctions were subjective and self-fulfilling: we met a better class of person where we stayed because we kept out of the way of the rest, Palm Court rather than bathing beauties, not the knobbly knees contest but a Wallace Arnold to Windermere. Package holidays came too late for my parents but had they ever ventured abroad they would have taken their attitudes with them. My mam would soon have located the Bispham end of Benidorm, a select part to Sitges. 'Well, we don't like it all hectic, do we, Dad?'

Common persists. It's not a distinction I'd want to be detected making but to myself I make it still. There are some lace (or more likely nylon) curtains popular nowadays that are gathered up for some reason in the middle. They look to me like a woman who's been to the lav and got her underskirt caught up behind her. They're absurd but that's not my real objection. They're common. The mock Georgian doorways that disfigure otherwise decent houses, the so-called Kentucky fried Georgian, offend me because they're cheap, inappropriate, ill-proportioned . . . and common.

Finally vicars who, Anglican though not always specified as such, turn up in all but one of these pieces, earnest, visitant and resolutely contemporary. Several are bearded, one is in trainers and most are in mufti. I have no particular wish to lock the clergy out of the wardrobe or ban them the boutique, but along with postmen and porters I wish they had not abandoned black. Just as postmen nowadays look like members of the Rumanian airforce so cassocks come in beige and even lilac, and if a parson submits to the indignity of a dog collar the chances are it has gone slimline, peeping coyly above a modish number in some fetching pastel shade. Nuns too have lost their old billowing, wimpled innocence and now look like prison wardresses on the loose. Even hearses have gone grey, black altogether too uncompromising a colour, life something to be shaded out of when, after much suffering tastefully borne, we blend nicely into the grave.

The clergy not wanting to look the part has something to do with the dismantling of the Book of Common Prayer. Anxious not to sound like parsons they can hardly be blamed for not wanting to look like them either. The 'underneath this cassock I am but a man like any other' act that Geoff does in *Bed Among the Lentils* must be a familiar routine at many a church door. And it's not of course new. Priests have always hankered after the world, or at any rate the worldly, and consorting as He did with publicans and sinners it was Jesus who started the rot. Or so Susan would say.

I don't know why it should be only Catholics who are thought never to escape their religious upbringing; I have never managed to outgrow mine. When I was sixteen and not long confirmed I was devoutly religious, a regular communicant who knew the service off by heart. It might be thought this would rejoice a vicar's heart and maybe it did, but actually I think the parish clergy found my fervour faintly embarrassing. A fervent Anglican is a bit of a contradiction in terms anyway, but I was conscious that my constant presence at the Eucharist, often midweek as well as Sundays, was thought to be rather unhealthy. As the celebrant sallied forth from the vestry on a cold winter's morning and found me sitting or (like Miss Frobisher, never one to let an opportunity slip) getting in a spot of silent prayer, he must have felt like a doctor opening the surgery door and discovering the sole occupant of the waiting room some tiresome hypochondriac (I was that too actually). Shy, bespectacled and innocent of the world I knew I was a disappointment to the clergy. What they wanted were brands to pluck from the burning and that was not me by a long chalk; I'd never even been near the fire.

Those early morning services with just a handful of regulars in the side chapel, the others generally maiden ladies who had cycled there on tall bicycles through the autumn mists, were to me the stuff of religion, the real taste of God. But though I did not admit it myself I knew that what the clergy preferred were occasions like Christmas Eve when the church was packed to the doors, the side aisles full, people even standing at the back like they did in those days at the cinema. For many in the congregation this was their one visit to church in the year. Plumping to my knees with split-second timing I would scornfully note how few of these festive communicants knew the service. Most of them didn't even kneel but sat, head in hand as if they were on the lavatory, this their one spiritual evacuation of the year.

Fastidious worshipper that I was, when I got to the altar rail I was even more choosy. Christmas and Easter, those joyous festivals of the Christian year, figured in my calendar as fearful health hazards and a true test of faith. At the sparsely attended eucharists that were the norm the rest of the year one could bank on finding oneself at the communion rail alongside a person of proven piety and blameless life. As my turn came for the chalice I would think of the TB or the cancer I might catch but come the Watch

Night services at Christmas and Easter these ailments were forgotten.
Then it was VD that was the bugbear. With the church chock-a-block with
publicans and sinners one never knew who was going to be one's drinking
companion. It was all my mother's fault. She had brought us up never to
share a lemonade bottle with other boys, and wiping it with your hand,
she said, was no protection, so I knew the dainty dab with the napkin the
priest gave the chalice made no difference at all. There was God of course,
in whose omnipotence I was supposed to believe: He might run to some
mystical antisepsis. But then He might not. That I should catch syphilis
from the chalice might be all part of His plan. The other place I was
frightened of contracting it was the seat of a public lavatory, and that the
rim of the toilet should be thus linked with the rim of the chalice was also
part of the wonderful mystery of God. It was on such questions of hygiene
rather than any of theology that my faith cut its teeth. I see myself walking
back from the altar and plunging to my knees, then at the first
opportunity surreptitiously spitting into my handkerchief. But I knew that
if God had marked me down for VD and a test of faith no amount of
spitting was going to help. It was all chickenfeed to the Ancient of Days.

Switching on the Test Match at Headingley by mistake nowadays, I see
the scene of these early spiritual struggles. 'Why, Headingley!' I might
say, parodying Larkin, 'I was re-born here.' The camera pans along the
Cardigan Road boundary and there above the trees is the spire of St
Michael's, designed by J.L. Pearson who built Truro Cathedral, St
Michael's with St Bartholomew's at Armley, the best of the nineteenth-
century churches in Leeds, and in those days I knew them all. Around the
time I was spitting into my handkerchief David Storey, the novelist and
playwright, was playing rugby for Wakefield and so was often on the
Headingley ground. For him too St Michael's was a symbol of hope. Cold,
wet and frightened in the middle of a game he would look longingly at the
spire and tell himself that within the hour he would be stood opposite the
church waiting for a tram; the match would be over and he would be
going home. That is by the way, but then so is much of this reminiscence,
my childhood itself fairly by the way, or so it seemed at the time. Brought
up in the provinces in the forties and fifties one learned early the valuable
lesson that life is generally something that happens elsewhere.

A Chip
in the Sugar

GRAHAM   Alan Bennett

Produced by Innes Lloyd
Directed by Stuart Burge
Designed by Tony Burrough
Music by George Fenton

Graham is a mild middle-aged man. The play is set in his bedroom, a small room with one window and one door. It is furnished with a single bed, a wardrobe, two chairs and nothing much else.

I'd just taken her tea up this morning when she said, 'Graham, I think the world of you.' I said, 'I think the world of you.' And she said, 'That's all right then.' I said, 'What's brought this on?' She said, 'Nothing. This tea looks strong, pull the curtains.' Of course I knew what had brought it on. She said, 'I wouldn't like you to think you're not Number One.' So I said, 'Well, you're Number One with me too. Give me your teeth. I'll swill them.'

What it was we'd had a spot of excitement yesterday: we ran into a bit of Mother's past. I said to her, 'I didn't know you had a past. I thought I was your past.' She said, 'You?' I said, 'Well, we go back a long way. How does he fit in vis-à-vis Dad?' She laughed. 'Oh, he was pre-Dad.' I said, 'Pre-Dad? I'm surprised you remember him, you don't remember to switch your blanket off.' She said, 'That's different. His name's Turnbull.' I said, 'I know. He said.'

I'd parked her by the war memorial on her usual seat while I went and got some reading matter. Then I waited while she went and spent a penny in the disabled toilet. She's not actually disabled, her memory's bad, but she says she prefers their toilets because you get more elbow room. She always takes for ever, diddling her hands and what not, and when she eventually comes back it turns out she's been chatting to the attendant. I said, 'What about?' She said, 'Hanging. She was in favour of stiffer penalties for minor offences and I thought, "Well, we know better, our Graham and me." I wish you'd been there, love; you could have given her the statistics, where are we going for our tea?'

The thing about Mam is that though she's never had a proper education, she's picked up enough from me to be able to hold her own in discussions about up-to-the-minute issues like the environment and the colour problem, and for a woman of her age and background she has a very liberal slant. She'll look at my *Guardian* and she actually thinks for herself. Doctor Chaudhury said to me, 'Full marks, Graham. The best way to avoid a broken hip is to have a flexible mind. Keep up the good work.'

They go mad round the war memorial so when we cross over I'll generally slip my arm through hers until we're safely across, only once we're on the pavement she'll postpone letting it go, because once upon a time we got stopped by one of these questionnaire women who reckons to take us for husband and wife. I mean, Mam's got white hair. She was doing this dodge and I said, 'Mam, let go of my arm.' I didn't really wrench it, only next thing I knew she's flat on the pavement. I said, 'Oh my God, Mother.'

People gather round and I pick up her bag, and she sits up and says, 'I've laddered both my stockings.' I said, 'Never mind your stockings, what about your pelvis?' She says, 'It's these bifocals. They tell you not to look down. I was avoiding some sick.' Somebody says, 'That's a familiar voice,' and there's a little fellow bending over her, green trilby hat, shorty raincoat. 'Hello,' he says, 'remember me?'

Well, she doesn't remember people, I know for a fact because she swore me down she'd never met Joy Buckle, who teaches Flowers in Felt and Fabric at my day centre. I said, 'You have met Joy, you knitted her a tea cosy.' That's all she can knit, tea cosies. And bed socks. Both outmoded articles. I said to her, 'Branch out. If you can knit tea cosies you can knit skiing hats.' She says, 'Well, I will.' Only I have to stand over her or else she'll still leave a hole for the spout. 'Anyway,' I said, 'you do remember Joy because you said she had some shocking eyebrows.' She said, 'I hope you didn't tell her that.' I said, 'Of course I didn't.' She said, 'Well, I don't remember.' And that's the way she is, she doesn't remember and here's this little fellow saying, 'Do you remember me?' So I said, 'No she won't. Come on, Mother. Let's get you up.' Only she says, 'Remember you? Of course. It's Frank Turnbull. It must be fifty years.' He said, 'Fifty-two. Filey. 1934.' She said, 'Sea-Crest.' He said, 'No sand in the bedrooms.' And they both cracked out laughing.

Meanwhile she's still stuck on the cold pavement. I said, 'Come along, Mother. We don't want piles.' Only he butts in again. He says, 'With respect, it's advisable not to move a person until it's been ascertained no bones are broken. I was in the St John's Ambulance Brigade.' 'Yes,' said Mother, 'and who did you learn your bandaging on?' And they both burst out laughing again. He had on these bright yellow gloves, could have been a bookie.

Eventually, I get my arms round her waist and hoist her up, only his lordship's no help as he claims to have a bad back. When I've finally got her restored to the perpendicular she introduces him. 'This is Frank Turnbull, a friend of mine from the old days.' What old days? First time I knew there were any old days. Turns out he's a gents' outfitter, semi-retired, shop in Bradford and some sort of outlet in Morecambe. I thought, 'Well, that accounts for the yellow gloves.'

Straight off he takes charge. He says, 'What you need now, Vera, is a cup of coffee.' I said, 'Well, we were just going for some tea, weren't we, Mother?' Vera! Her name's not Vera. She's never been called Vera. My Dad never called her Vera, except just once, when they were wheeling him into the theatre. Vera. 'Right,' he says, 'follow me.' And puts his arm through hers. 'Careful,' she says. 'You'll make my boy friend jealous.' I didn't say anything.

Pause.

Now the café we generally patronise is just that bit different. It's plain but it's classy, no cloths on the tables, the menu comes on a little slate and the waitresses wear their own clothes and look as if they're doing it just for the fun of it. The stuff's all home-made and we're both big fans of the date and walnut bread. I said, 'This is the place.' Mr Turnbull goes straight past. 'No,' he says, 'I know somewhere, just opened. Press on.'

Now, if there's one thing Mother and me are agreed on it's that red is a common colour. And the whole place is done out in red. Lampshades red. Waitresses in red. Plates red, and on the tables those plastic sauce things got up to look like tomatoes. Also red. And when I look there's a chip in the sugar. I thought, 'Mother won't like this.' 'Oh,' she says, 'this looks cheerful, doesn't it, Graham?' I said, 'There's a chip in the sugar.' 'A detail,' he says, 'they're still having their teething troubles. Is it three coffees?' I said, 'We like tea,' only Mother says, 'No. I feel like an adventure. I'll have coffee.' He gets hold of the menu and puts his hand on hers. 'Might I suggest,' he says, 'a cheeseburger?' She said, 'Oh, what's that?' He said, 'It's fresh country beef, mingled with golden-fried onions, topped off with toasted cheese served with french fries and lemon wedge.' 'Oh, lemon wedge,' said Mother. 'That sounds nice.' I thought, 'Well, I hope you can keep it down.' Because it'll be the pizza story all over again. One mouthful and at four o'clock in the morning I was still stuck at her bedside with the bucket. She said, 'I like new experiences in eating. I had a pizza once, didn't I, Graham?' I didn't say anything.

They fetch the food and she's wiring in. He said, 'Are you enjoying your cheeseburger?' She said, 'I am. Would I be mistaken in thinking that's tomato sauce?' He said, 'It is.' She says, 'Give us a squirt.' They both burst out laughing. He said, 'Glass cups, Graham. Be careful or we'll see up your nose.' More laughter. She said, 'Graham's quite refined. He often has a dry sherry.'

'Well, he could do with smartening up a bit,' Mr Turnbull said. 'Plastic mac. He wants one of these quilted jobs, I've shifted a lot of those.' 'I don't like those quilted jobs,' I said. 'He sweats,' Mother said. 'There's no excuse for that in this day and age,' Mr Turnbull said, 'the range of preparations there are on the market. You want to invest in some roll-on deodorant.' Everybody could hear. 'And flares are anathema even in Bradford.'

'Graham doesn't care, do you, Graham?' Mother said. 'He reads a lot.' 'So what?' Mr Turnbull said. 'I know several big readers who still manage to be men about town. Lovat green's a nice shade. I tell you this, Graham,' he said, 'if I were squiring a young lady like this around town I wouldn't do it in grey socks and sandals. These shoes are Italian. Feel.' 'I always think Graham would have made a good parson,' Mother said, feeling his foot, 'only he doesn't believe in God.' 'That's no handicap these days,' Mr Turnbull said. 'What do you do?'

'He's between jobs at present,' Mother said, 'He used to do soft toys for handicapped children. Then he was making paper flowers at one stage.' I went to the toilet.

Pause.

When I came back he said, 'I don't believe in mental illness. Nine times out of ten it's a case of pulling your socks up.' I didn't say anything. Mother said, 'Yes, well, I think the pendulum's gone too far.' She didn't look at me. 'It's like these girls, not eating,' he said, 'they'd eat if they'd been brought up like us, Vera, nothing to eat.' 'That's right,' Mother said, 'they have it too easy. Did you marry?' 'Twice,' he said. 'I buried Amy last May. I was heartbroken but life has to go on. I've a son lives in Stevenage. I've got two grandsons, one at the motorbike stage. Do you drive?' 'No,' I said. 'You do,' Mother said. 'You had that scooter.' 'It was only a moped,' I said. 'Well, a moped, Graham. They're all the same. I can't get him to blow his own trumpet.'

'I've got a Rover 2000,' Mr Turnbull said, 'handles like a dream. I think the solution to mental illness is hard physical work. Making raffia mats, I'd go mad.' 'Yes,' says Mother, 'only they do pottery as well. I've seen some nice ashtrays.' 'Featherbedding,' Mr Turnbull said. 'Do you like these Pakistanis?' 'Well, in moderation,' Mother said. 'We have a nice newsagent. Graham thinks we're all the same.' I said, 'I thought you did.' She said, 'Well, I do when you explain it all to me, Graham, but then I forget the explanation and I'm back to square one.' 'There is no explanation,' Mr Turnbull said. 'They sell mangoes in our post office, what explanation is there for that?' 'I know,' Mother said,' I smelled curry on my *Woman's Own*. You have to be educated to understand.' I didn't say anything.

He ran us home, promised to give her a tinkle next time he was in the neighbourhood. Said he was often round here tracking down two-tone cardigans. 'Your Mother's a grand woman,' he said. 'You want to cherish her.' 'He does, he does,' Mother said. 'You're my boy friend, aren't you, Graham?' She put her arm through mine.

Go to black.

Come up on Graham standing looking out of the window. It is late afternoon. He sits on the arm of the chair.

There must be a famine on somewhere because we were just letting our midday meal go down when the vicar calls with some envelopes. Breezes in, anorak and running shoes, and he says, 'I always look forward to coming to this house, Mrs Whittaker.' (He's got the idea she's deaf, which she's not; it's one of the few things she isn't.) He says, 'Do you know why? It's because you two remind me of Jesus and his mother.' Well, I've always thought Jesus was a bit off-hand with his mother, and on one occasion I remember he was quite snotty with her, but I didn't say anything. And of course Madam is over the moon. In her book if you can't get compared with the Queen Mother the Virgin Mary's the next best thing. She says, 'Are you married?' (She asks him every time, never remembers.) He said, 'No, Mrs Whittaker. I am married to God.' She says, 'Where does that leave you with the housework?' He said, 'Well, I don't do as well as your Graham. He's got this place like a palace.' She says, 'Well, I do my whack. I washed four pairs of stockings this morning.' She hadn't. She put them in the bowl then they slipped her mind, so the rest of the operation devolved on me.

He said, 'How are you today, Mrs Whittaker?' She says, 'Stiff down one side.' I said, 'She had a fall yesterday.' She says, 'I never did.' I said, 'You did, Mother. You had a fall, then you ran into Mr Turnbull.'

Pause.

She says, 'That's right. I did.' And she starts rooting in her bag for her
lipstick. She says, 'That's one of them anoraky things, isn't it? They've
gone out now, those. If you want to look like a man about town you want
to get one of those continental quilts.' He said, 'Oh?' I said, 'She means
those quilted jackets.' She said, 'He knows what I mean. Where did you
get those shoes?' He said, 'They're training shoes.' She said, 'Training for
what? Are you not fully qualified?' He said, 'If Jesus were alive today,
Mrs Whittaker, I think you'd find these were the type of shoes he would
be wearing.' 'Not if his mother had anything to do with it,' she said.
'She'd have him down Stead and Simpson's and get him into some good
brogues. Somebody was telling me the Italians make good shoes.'

   The vicar takes this as his cue to start on about people who have no
shoes at all and via this to the famine in Ethiopia. I fork out 50p which he
says will feed six families for a week and she says, 'Well, it would have
bought me some Quality Street.' When he's at the door he says, 'I take my
hat off to you, Graham, I've got a mother myself.' When I get back in she
said, 'Vicar! He looked more like the paper boy. How can you look up to
somebody in pumps?' Just then there's a knock at the door. 'Get down,'
she says, 'he's back.' Only it isn't. It's Mr Turnbull.

   Graham stands up.

New outfit this time: little suede coat, corduroy collar, maroon trousers.
She says, 'You're colourful.' 'We just happen to have these slacks on
offer,' he says. 'I was wondering whether you fancied a run out to Bolton
Abbey?' 'Bolton Abbey?' she says. 'Oh, that's right up our street, isn't it,
Graham? Graham's good with buildings, aren't you, Graham? He knows all
the periods of houses. There's one period that's just come in. Other people
don't like it yet but we do, don't we, Graham?' 'I don't know,' I said.
'You do. What is it?' 'Victorian,' I said. 'That's it, Victorian. Only
there's a lot been pulled down.' Mr Turnbull yawns. 'I've got a little
bungalow.' 'That's nice,' Mother says. 'I like a nice bungalow, don't you,
Graham?' 'Yes,' I said, 'provided it's not a blot on the landscape.'
'Mine's architect designed,' says Mr Turnbull. 'It has a patio and a
breakfast bar, it overlooks a beauty spot.' 'Oh,' said Mother, 'sounds tip-
top. We'd better be getting our skates on, Graham.' He said, 'I've got to
pick up a load of green three-quarter-length windcheaters in Ilkley; there
won't really be room for a third party. Isn't there anything on at the
pictures?' 'Oh he'll be happy reading,' Mother said. 'Won't you,

Graham?' 'Anyway,' Mr Turnbull said, 'you don't always want to be with your Mother at your age, do you, Graham?' I didn't say anything.

He sits on the chair arm again.

I've been laid on my bed reading one of my magazines. I've a feeling that somebody's looking at the house, only I can't see anybody. Once or twice I think I've heard a knock on the door, but I haven't gone in case there's nobody there.

Go to black.

Come up on Graham sitting on his unmade bed in his pyjamas. Night.

Today they went over to York. It was after seven when he dropped her off. He generally comes in but not this time. Just gives her a little kiss. She has to bend down. I said, 'Have you had a good time?' She said, 'Yes. We had egg and chips, tea, bread and butter, we've got a lot in common and there's a grand new car park.' I said, 'Did you go in the Minster?' She said, 'No. Frank's not keen on old buildings. We need to look more to the future. He says they've built a spanking new precinct in Bradford, so that's going to be next on the agenda. You're quiet.' I said, 'Well, do you wonder? Doctor Chaudhury says I should have a stable environment. This isn't a stable environment with your fancy men popping in every five minutes.' She said, 'He isn't my fancy man.' I said, 'Well, he's your fancy man in embryo.' She said, 'You know I don't know what that means.' I said, 'How old are you?' She said, 'I don't know.' I said, 'You do know.' She said, 'I don't. Tell me.' I said, 'You're seventy-two.' 'That's not so old. How old was Winston Churchill?' I said, 'When?' She said, 'You think you've got it over me, Graham Whittaker. Well, I'll tell you something, my memory's better with Frank. He was telling me about the economy. You've got it all wrong.' I said, 'How?' 'I can't remember but you have. Blaming it on the government. Frank says it's the blacks.' I didn't say anything, just came upstairs.

When I went down again she's still sat there with her hat and coat on. I said: 'Do you want to knit him a tea cosy?' She said, 'I don't think he's the tea-cosy type. When I first knew him he had a motorbike and sidecar. Besides, I think it's got beyond the tea-cosy stage.' I said, 'What do you mean?' She said, 'Graham. My one aim in life is for you to be happy. If I thought that by dying I would make you happy I would.' I said, 'Mother,

your dying wouldn't make me happy. In fact the reverse. It would make me unhappy. Anyway, Mother, you're not going to die.' She said, 'No. I'm not going to die. I'm going to get married. And the honeymoon is in Tenerife. Have one of your tablets.'

She made a cup of tea. I said, 'How can you go to Tenerife, you're smothered at Scarborough?' She said, 'It's a four-star hotel with tip-top air-conditioning, you get your breakfast from a long table.' I said, 'What about your bowels?' She said, 'What about my bowels?' 'Well, you said they were unpredictable at Morecambe. Get them to the Canary Islands and they're going to be all over the place.' She said, 'Who's talking about the Canary Islands? I'm going to Tenerife.' 'And what about post-Tenerife? Where are you going to live?' She said, 'Here. Frank says he'll be away on and off on business but he wants to call this home.' I said, 'What about me?' She went into the kitchen. 'Well, we wondered whether you'd prefer to go back to the hostel. You were happy at the hostel. You rubbed shoulders with all sorts.' I said, 'Mam. This is my home.' She said, 'A man shouldn't be living with his mother at your age, Frank says. Did you take a tablet?'

Now it's four o'clock in the morning and I can't sleep. There's a car parked outside. I can't see but I think there's somebody in it, watching like they used to do before. I thought all that chapter was closed.

Go to black.

Come up on Graham sitting on an upright chair. Evening.

This morning I went to Community Caring down at the Health Centre. It caters for all sorts. Steve, who runs it, is dead against what he calls 'the ghetto approach'. What he's after is a nice mix of personality difficulties as being the most fruitful exercise in problem-solving and a more realistic model of society generally. There's a constant flow of coffee, 'oiling the wheels' Steve calls it, and we're all encouraged to ventilate our problems and generally let our hair down. I sometimes feel a bit out of it as I've never had any particular problems, so this time when Steve says 'Now chaps and chappesses who's going to set the ball rolling?' I get in quick and tell them about Mother and Mr Turnbull. When I'd finished Steve said, 'Thank you, Graham, for sharing your problem with us. Does anybody want to kick it around?'

First off the mark is Leonard, who wonders whether Graham has sufficiently appreciated that old people can fall in love and have meaningful relationships generally, the same as young people. I suppose this is understandable coming from Leonard because he's sixty-five, only he doesn't have meaningful relationships. He's been had up for exposing himself in Sainsbury's doorway. As Mother said, 'Tesco, you could understand it.'

Then Janice chips in. 'Had they been having sexual intercourse?' I said I didn't want to think about it. Steve said, 'Why?' I said I didn't know. So he said, 'Maybe what we should be talking about is why Graham is being so defensive about sexual intercourse.' I said, 'Steve. I am not being defensive about sexual intercourse. She is my mother.' Jackie, who's nine parts Lesbian, said, 'Graham. She is also A Woman.' I couldn't believe this. I said, 'Jackie. You're an ex-battered wife. I thought you didn't approve of marriage.' She said, 'Graham. I approve of caring marriage.' I said, 'Jackie. This is not caring marriage.' She said, 'Graham, what's Tenerife? That's caring. All I got was a black eye and a day trip to Fleetwood.' Then they all have a go. Get Graham. Steve summed up. 'The general feeling of the group is that Graham could be more open.' I said,

'How can I be more open? There's somebody sat outside the house watching.' I wanted to discuss that only Leonard leaped in and said he felt the need to talk through an episode behind British Home Stores. I stuck it a bit longer and then came home.

Mother's sat there, all dolled up. Earrings on, chiffon scarf, lathered in make-up. She said, 'Oh, I thought you were Mr Turnbull.' I said, 'No.' She said, 'I'll just go to the lav.' She goes three times in the next ten minutes. I said, 'You're not getting married today, are you?' She said, 'No. There's a new Asda superstore opened at Bingley and we thought we'd give it the once over. Frank says they have a very good selection of sun tan lotions.' I said, 'Mother, there's somebody watching the house.' She said, 'I want to pick out some tissues and Frank's looking for a little chammy for his windscreen. He's promised me something called a cheeseburger, there's a café that's part of the complex.'

Just then there's a little toot on the horn and she runs to the lav again. I said, 'Don't go. Don't leave me, Mam.' She said, 'I'm not giving in to you, you're a grown man. Is my underskirt showing?' He toots again. She says, 'Look at your magazines, make yourself a poached egg.' I said, 'Mam.' She said, 'There's that bit of chicken in the fridge. You could iron those two vests. Take a tablet. Give us a kiss. Toodle pip.'

I thought I'd go sit in the back room where they couldn't see me. I pulled the curtains and I'm sitting there in the dark and I think I hear a knock at the front door. I don't move and there's another knock. Louder. I do like Doctor Chaudhury says and tell myself it's not happening, only it is. Somebody shouts through the letter-box. 'I know you're in there. Open this door.' So I do. And there is someone. It's a woman.

She said, 'Are you the son?' I said, 'What?' She said, 'Are you the son? I'm the daughter.' I said, 'Have you been watching the house?' She said, 'On and off. Why?' I said, 'Nothing.' She said, 'I don't know what there is to look so suited about.' I said, 'You'd better come in.'

Go to black.

Come up on Graham as he puts a magazine on top of the wardrobe. He sits down in the easy chair. Night.

It's nine o'clock when I hear the car outside. I'm sitting watching TV. I say, 'Oh hello. Did you have a nice time?' She said, 'Yes. Yes we did, thank you.' 'Did you get your sun tan lotion?' She said, 'What sun tan lotion?'

'You were going to get some sun tan lotion. Never mind. You've forgotten. How's Mr Turnbull?' 'Frank? He's all right.' She took her things off. 'I'm sure you could get to like him, Graham, if only you got to know him.' I said, 'Well, you should have brought him in.' 'Well, I will next time. It'd be nice if now and again we could go off as a threesome. What have you done?' 'Nothing,' I said. 'Just sat here.' 'You've been all right?' 'Mmm.'

'You see,' she said, 'there wasn't anybody outside.' 'Oh yes there was.' She said, 'Oh Graham. Have you had a tablet? Have a tablet.' 'I don't want a tablet. I'll tell you who was sat outside. Mrs Pamela Musgrave.' She said, 'Who's she?' 'Née Turnbull. The daughter of your hubby to be.' She said, 'He hasn't got a daughter. He's got a son down south. He hasn't got a daughter,' she said, 'you're making stuff up now, have a tablet.' I said, 'I'm not making it up. And there's something else I'm not making up. Mrs Turnbull.' She said, 'There isn't a Mrs Turnbull. She's dead. I'm going to the lav.' I said, 'She's not dead. She's in a wheelchair with a broken heart. He's been having you on.'

After a bit she comes out. 'You're just saying all this.' 'The number's on the pad. Ring up. She's disabled is his wife. Has been for ten years. Their daughter looks after them. You're not the first. He's always doing it. One woman, it was going to be Barbados. Somebody spotted you together at Bolton Abbey. A well-wisher. Tenerife!'

Later on I took her a cup of tea. She'd been crying. She said, 'I bought this little bedjacket.' I said, 'I'm sorry, Mam.' She said, 'He was right enough. What can you expect at my age? How old am I?' 'Seventy-two.' 'That's another thing. I remembered with him. I don't remember with you.' I said, 'I'm sorry.' She said, 'You're not sorry. How are you sorry? You didn't like him.' I said, 'He wasn't good enough for you.' She said, 'I'm the best judge of that. He was natty, more than can be said for you.' And starts crying again. I said, 'I understand, Mam.' She said, 'You don't understand. How can you understand, you, you're not normal?' I said, 'I'm going to bed.'

In a bit she comes shouting outside the door. 'You think you've got it over me, Graham Whittaker. Well, you haven't. I've got it over you.' I said, 'Go back to bed.' She said, 'I know the kind of magazines you read.' I said, 'Chess. You'll catch cold.' She said, 'They never are chess. Chess with no clothes on. Chess in their birthday suits. That kind of chess. Chess men.' I said, 'Go to bed. And turn your blanket off.'

Pause.

Next day she's right as rain. Forgotten it. Never mentions it anyway, except just as we're coming out of the house she said, 'I do love you, Graham.' I said, 'I love you too.' She said, 'Anyway he had a hearing aid.' She said, 'What's on the agenda for today, then?' I said, 'I thought we might have a little ride to Ripon.' She said, 'Oh yes, Ripon. That's nice. We could go to the cathedral. We like old buildings, don't we, you and me?'

She put her arm through mine.

Fade out.

Bed Among the Lentils

SUSAN   Maggie Smith

Produced by Innes Lloyd
Directed by Alan Bennett
Designed by Tony Burrough
Music by George Fenton

Susan is a vicar's wife. She is thin and nervous and probably smokes. She sits on an upright chair in the kitchen. It is evening.

Geoffrey's bad enough but I'm glad I wasn't married to Jesus. The lesson this morning was the business in the Garden of Gethsemane when Jesus prays and the disciples keep falling asleep. He wakes them up and says, 'Could you not watch with me one hour?' It's my mother.

I overslept this morning, flung on a cardigan and got there just as everybody was standing up. It was Holy Communion so the militants were out in force, the sub-zero temperature in the side-chapel doubtless adding to the attraction.

Geoffrey kicks off by apologising for his failure to de-frost the church. (Subdued merriment.) Mr Medlicott has shingles, Geoffrey explains, and, as is well known, has consistently refused to initiate us lesser mortals into the mysteries of the boiler. (Helpless laughter.)

Mrs Belcher read the lesson. Mr Belcher took the plate round. 'Big day for you,' I said to them afterwards.

The sermon was about sex. I didn't actually nod off, though I have heard it before. Marriage gives the OK to sex is the gist of it, but while it is far from being the be all and end all (you can say that again) sex is nevertheless the supreme joy of the married state and a symbol of the relationship between us and God. So, Geoffrey concludes, when we put our money in the plate it is a symbol of everything in our lives we are offering to God and that includes our sex. I could only find 10p.

Thinking about the sermon during the hymn I felt a pang of sympathy for the Deity, gifted with all this sex. No fun being made a present of the rare and desiccated conjunctions that take place between Geoffrey and me. Or the frightful collisions that presumably still occur between the Belchers. Not to mention whatever shamefaced fumblings go on between Miss Budd and Miss Bantock. 'It's all right if we offer it to God, Alice.' 'Well, if you say so, Pauline.'

Amazing scenes at the church door. Geoffrey had announced that after Easter the bishop would be paying us a visit so the fan club were running round in small circles, Miss Frobisher even going so far as to squeeze my elbow. Meanwhile, Geoffrey stands there the wind billowing out his surplice and ruffling his hair, what 'Who's Who in the Diocese of Ripon' calls 'his schoolboy good looks'. I helped put away the books while he did his 'underneath this cassock I am but a man like anybody else' act. 'Such

a live wire,' said Mrs Belcher, 'really putting the parish on the map.'
'That's right,' burbles Mrs Shrubsole, looking at me. 'We must cherish
him.'

We came back and I cherished him with some chicken wings in a tuna
fish sauce. He said, 'That went down well.' I said, 'The chicken wings?'
He said, 'My sermon. I felt it hit the nail on the head.' He put his hand
over mine, hoping, I suppose, that having hit one nail he might hit
another, but I said I had to go round with the parish magazine. 'Good
girl,' he said. 'I can attack my paperwork instead.'

Roads busy. Sunday afternoon. Families having a run out. Wheeling the
pram, walking the dog. Living. Almighty God unto whom all hearts be
open, and from whom no secrets are hid, cleanse the thoughts of our hearts
by the inspiration of thy holy spirit that we may perfectly love thee and
worthily magnify thy glorious name and not spend our Sunday afternoons
parked in a lay-by on the Ring Road wondering what happened to our life.

When I got back Geoffrey was just off to Evensong, was I going to
come? When I said 'No' he said, 'Really? Then I'd better pretend you
have a headache.'

Why? One of the unsolved mysteries of life, or the unsolved mysteries
of my life, is why the vicar's wife is expected to go to church at all. A
barrister's wife doesn't have to go to court, an actor's wife isn't at every
performance, so why have I always got to be on parade? Not to mention
the larger question of whether one believes in God in the first place. It's
assumed that being the vicar's wife one does but the question has never
actually come up, not with Geoffrey anyway. I can understand why, of
course. To look at me, the hair, the flat chest, the wan smile, you'd think
I was just cut out for God. And maybe I am. I'd just like to have been
asked that's all. Not that it matters of course. So long as you can run a
tight jumble sale you can believe in what you like.

It could be that Geoffrey doesn't believe in God either. I've always
longed to ask him only God never seems to crop up. 'Geoffrey,' I'd say.
'Yes, Susan?' 'Do you really believe in God? I mean, cards on tables, you
don't honestly, do you? God's just a job like any other. You've got to
bring home the bacon somehow.' But no. Not a word. The subject's never
discussed.

After he'd gone I discovered we were out of sherry so I've just been
round to the off-licence. The woman served me. Didn't smile. I can't
think why. I spend enough.

Go to black.

Come up on Susan on the steps of the side-chapel, polishing a candlestick. Afternoon.

We were discussing the ordination of women. The bishop asked me what I thought. Should women take the services? So long as it doesn't have to be me, I wanted to say, they can be taken by a trained gorilla. 'Oh yes,' Geoffrey chips in, 'Susan's all in favour. She's keener than I am, aren't you, darling?' 'More sprouts anybody?' I said.

On the young side for a bishop, but he's been a prominent sportsman at university so that would explain it. Boxing or rugby. Broken nose at some stage anyway. One of the 'Christianity is common sense' brigade. Hobby's bricklaying apparently and refers to me throughout as 'Mrs Vicar'. Wants beer with his lunch and Geoffrey says he'll join him so this leaves me with the wine. Geoffrey's all over him because the rumour is he's shopping round for a new Archdeacon. Asks Geoff how outgoing I am. Actually says that. 'How outgoing is Mrs Vicar?' Mr Vicar jumps in with a quick rundown of my accomplishments and an outline of my punishing schedule. On a typical day, apparently, I kick off by changing the wheel on the Fiesta, then hasten to the bedside of a dying pensioner, after which, having done the altar flowers and dispensed warmth and appreciation to sundry parishioners en route, I top off a thrill-packed morning by taking round Meals on Wheels . . . somehow – 'and this to me is the miracle,' says Geoffrey – 'somehow managing to rustle up a delicious lunch in the interim', the miracle somewhat belied by the flabby lasagna we are currently embarked on. 'The ladies,' says the bishop. 'Where would we be without them?'

Disaster strikes as I'm doling out the tinned peaches: the jug into which I've decanted the Carnation milk gets knocked over, possibly by me. Geoffrey, for whom turning the other cheek is part of the job, claims it caught his elbow and his lordship takes the same line, insisting he gets doused in Carnation milk practically every day of his life. Still, when I get a dishcloth and sponge off his gaiters I catch him giving me a funny look. It's Mary Magdalen and the Nivea cream all over again. After lunch Geoffrey's supposed to be taking him on a tour of the parish but while we're having a cup of instant he claps his hand to his temple because he's suddenly remembered he's supposed to be in Keighley blessing a steam engine.

We're stacking the dishwasher and I ask Geoffrey how he thinks it's gone. Doesn't know. 'Fingers crossed,' I say. 'I think there are more constructive things we could do than that,' he says crisply, and goes off to mend his inner tube. I sit by the Aga for a bit and as I doze off it comes to me that by 'constructive things' he perhaps means prayer.

When I wake up there's a note from Geoffrey. 'Gone to talk to the Ladies Bright Hour. Go to bed.' I'm not sleepy and anyway we're running low on sherry so I drive into Leeds. I've stopped going round the corner now as I owe them a bit on the side and she's always so surly. There's a little Indian shop behind the Infirmary I've found. It's a newsagents basically but it sells drink and anything really, the way they do. Open last thing at night, Sundays included, my ideal. Ramesh he's called. Mr Ramesh I call him, though Ramesh may be his Christian name. Only not Christian of course. I've been once or twice now, only this time he sits me in the back place on a sack of something and talks. Little statuette of a god on the wall. A god. Not The God. Not the definite article. One of several thousand apparently. 'Safety in numbers,' I said but he didn't understand. Looks a bit more fun than Jesus anyway. Shows me pictures of other gods, getting up to all sorts. I said, 'She looks a very busy lady. Is that yoga?' He said, 'Well, it helps.' He's quite athletic himself apparently, married, but his wife's only about fourteen so they won't let her in. He calls me Mrs Vicar too, only it's different. He has lovely teeth.

Go to black.

Come up on Susan in the kitchen near the Aga. Morning.

Once upon a time I had my life planned out . . . or half of it at any rate. I wasn't clear about the first part, but at the stroke of fifty I was all set to turn into a wonderful woman . . . the wife to a doctor, or a vicar's wife, Chairman of the Parish Council, a pillar of the WI. A wise, witty and ultimately white-haired old lady, who's always stood on her own feet until one day at the age of eighty she comes out of the County Library, falls under the weight of her improving book, breaks her hip and dies peacefully, continently and without fuss under a snowy coverlet in the cottage hospital. And coming away from her funeral in a country churchyard on a bright winter's afternoon people would say, 'Well, she was a wonderful woman.'

Had this been a serious ambition I should have seen to it I was equipped with the skills necessary to its achievement. How to produce jam which, after reaching a good, rolling boil, successfully coats the spoon; how to whip up a Victoria sponge that just gives to the fingertips; how to plan, execute and carry through a successful garden fête. All weapons in the armoury of any upstanding Anglican lady. But I can do none of these things. I'm even a fool at the flower arrangement. I ought to have a PhD in the subject the number of classes I've been to but still my efforts show as much evidence of art as walking sticks in an umbrella stand. Actually it's temperament. I don't have it. If you think squash is a competitive activity try flower arrangement.

On this particular morning the rota has Miss Frobisher and Mrs Belcher down for the side aisles and I'm paired with Mrs Shrubsole to do the altar and the lectern. My honest opinion, never voiced needless to say, is that if they were really sincere about religion they'd forget flower arrangement altogether, invest in some permanent plastic jobs and put the money towards the current most popular famine. However, around mid-morning I wander over to the church with a few dog-eared chrysanthemums. They look as if they could do with an immediate drink so I call in at the vestry and root out a vase or two from the cupboard where Geoffrey keeps the communion wine.

It not looming very large on my horizon, I assume I am doing the altar and Mrs Shrubsole the lectern, but when I come out of the vestry Mrs S is at the altar well embarked on her arrangement. I said, 'I thought I was doing the altar.' She said, 'No. I think Mrs Belcher will bear me out. I'm down to do the altar. You are doing the lectern. Why?' She smiled sweetly. 'Do you have a preference?' The only preference I have is to shove my chrysanthemums up her nose but instead I practise a bit of Christian forbearance and go stick them in a vase by the lectern. In the best tradition of my floral arrangements they look like the poles of a wigwam, so I go and see if I can cadge a bit of backing from Mrs Belcher. 'Are you using this?' I say, picking up a bit of mouldy old fern. 'I certainly am. I need every bit of my spiraea. It gives it body.' I go over and see if Miss Frobisher has any greenery going begging only she's doing some Japanese number, a vase like a test-tube half filled with gravel, in which she's throttling a lone carnation. So I retire to the vestry for a bit to calm my shattered nerves, and when I come out ready to tackle my chrysanths again Mrs Shrubsole has apparently finished and fetched the

other two up to the altar to admire her handiwork. So I wander up and take a look.

Well, it's a brown job, beech leaves, teazles, grass, that school of thought. Mrs Shrubsole is saying, 'It's called Forest Murmurs. It's what I did for my Highly Commended at Harrogate last year. What do you think?' Gert and Daisy are of course speechless with admiration, but when I tentatively suggest it might look a bit better if she cleared up all the bits and pieces lying around she said, 'What bits and pieces?' I said, 'All these acorns and fir-cones and what not. What's this conker in aid of?' She said, 'Leave that. The whole arrangement pivots on that.' I said, 'Pivots?' 'When the adjudicator was commenting on my arrangement he particularly singled out the hint I gave of the forest floor.' I said, 'Mrs Shrubsole. This is the altar of St Michael and All Angels. It is not The Wind in the Willows.' Mrs Belcher said, 'I think you ought to sit down.' I said, 'I do not want to sit down.' I said, 'It's all very well to transform the altar into something out of Bambi but do not forget that for the vicar the altar is his working surface. Furthermore,' I added, 'should the vicar sink to his knees in prayer, which since this is the altar he is wont to do, he is quite likely to get one of these teazle things in his eye. This is not a flower arrangement. It is a booby trap. A health hazard. In fact,' I say in a moment of supreme inspiration, 'it should be labelled HAZFLOR. Permit me to demonstrate.' And I begin getting down on my knees just to prove how lethal her bloody Forest Murmurs is. Only I must have slipped because next thing I know I'm rolling down the altar steps and end up banging my head on the communion rail.

Mrs Shrubsole, who along with every other organisation known to man has been in the St John's Ambulance Brigade, wants me left lying down, whereas Mrs Belcher is all for getting me on to a chair. 'Leave them lying down,' says Mrs Belcher, 'and they inhale their own vomit. It happens all the time, Veronica.' 'Only, Muriel,' says Mrs Shrubsole, 'when they have vomited. She hasn't vomited.' 'No,' I say, 'but I will if I have to listen to any more of this drivel,' and begin to get up. 'Is that blood, Veronica?' says Mrs Belcher pointing to my head. 'Well,' says Mrs Shrubsole, reluctant to concede to Mrs B on any matter remotely touching medicine, 'it could be, I suppose. What we need is some hot sweet tea.' 'I thought that theory had been discredited,' says Mrs Belcher. Discredited or not it sends Miss Frobisher streaking off to find a teabag, and also, it subsequently transpires, to telephone all and sundry in an effort to locate Geoffrey. He is in York taking part in the usual interdenominational conference on the role of the church in a hitherto uncolonised department of life, underfloor central heating possibly. He comes haring back thinking I'm at death's door, and finding I'm not has nothing more constructive to offer than I take a nap.

This gives the fan club the green light to invade the vicarage, making endless tea and the vicar his lunch and, as he puts it, 'spoiling him rotten'. Since this also licenses them to conduct a fact-finding survey of all the housekeeping arrangements or absence of same ('Where does she keep the Duroglit, vicar?'), a good time is had by all. Meanwhile Emily Brontë is laid out on the sofa in a light doze.

I come round to hear Geoffrey saying, 'Mrs Shrubsole's going now, darling.' I don't get up. I never even open my eyes. I just wave and say, 'Goodbye, Mrs Shrubsole.' Only thinking about it as I drift off again I think I may have said, 'Goodbye, Mrs Subsoil.' Anyway I meant the other. Shrubsoil.

When I woke up it was dark and Geoffrey'd gone out. I couldn't find a thing in the cupboard so I got the car out and drove into Leeds. I sat in the shop for a bit, not saying much. Then I felt a bit wanny and Mr Ramesh let me go into the back place to lie down. I must have dozed off because when I woke up Mr Ramesh has come in and started taking off his clothes. I said, 'What are you doing? What about the shop?' He said, 'Do not worry about the shop. I have closed the shop.' I said, 'It's only nine. You don't close till eleven.' 'I do tonight,' he said. I said, 'What's tonight?' He said, 'A chance in a million. A turn-up for the books. Will you take your clothes off please.' And I did.

Go to black.

Come up on Susan sitting in the vestry having a cigarette. Afternoon.

You never see pictures of Jesus smiling, do you? I mentioned this to Geoffrey once. 'Good point, Susan,' is what he said, which made me wish I'd not brought it up in the first place. Said I should think of Our Lord as having an inward smile, the doctrine according to Geoffrey being that Jesus was made man so he smiled, laughed and did everything else just like the rest of us. 'Do you think he ever smirked?' I asked, whereupon Geoffrey suddenly remembered he was burying somebody in five minutes and took himself off.

If Jesus *is* all man I just wish they'd put a bit more of it into the illustrations. I was sitting in church yesterday, wrestling with this point of theology, when it occurred to me that something seemed to have happened to Geoffrey. The service should have kicked off ages ago but he's still in the vestry. Mr Bland is filling in with something uplifting on the organ and Miss Frobisher, never one to let an opportunity slip, has slumped to her knees for a spot of unscheduled silent prayer. Mrs Shrubsole is lost in contemplation of the altar, still adorned with Forest Murmurs, a trail of ivy round the cross the final inspired touch. Mr Bland now ups the volume but still no sign of Geoff. 'Arnold,' says Mrs Belcher, 'there seems to be some hiatus in the proceedings,' and suddenly the fan club is on red alert. She's just levering him to his feet when I get in first and nip in there to investigate.

His reverence is there, white-faced, every cupboard open and practically in tears. He said, 'Have you seen it?' I said, 'What?' He said, 'The wine. The communion wine. It's gone.' I said, 'That's no tragedy,' and offer to pop out and get some ordinary. Geoffrey said, 'They're not open. Besides, what does it look like?' I said, 'Well, it looks like we've run out of communion wine.' He said, 'We haven't run out. There was a full bottle here on Friday. Somebody has drunk it.'

It's on the tip of my tongue to say that if Jesus is all he's cracked up to be why doesn't he use tap-water and put it to the test when I suddenly remember that Mr Bland keeps a bottle of cough mixture in his cupboard in case any of the choirboys gets chesty. At the thought of celebrating the Lord's Supper in Benylin Geoffrey now has a complete nervous breakdown but, as I point out, it's red and sweet and nobody is going to notice. Nor do they. I see Mr Belcher licking his lips a bit thoughtfully as he walks back down the aisle but that's all. 'What was the delay?' asks Mrs Shrubsole. 'Nothing,' I said, 'just a little hiccup.'

Having got it right for once I'm feeling quite pleased with myself, but Geoffrey obviously isn't and never speaks all afternoon so I bunk off Evensong and go into Leeds.

Mr Ramesh has evidently been expecting me because there's a bed made up in the storeroom upstairs. I go up first and get in. When I'm in bed I can put my hand out and feel the lentils running through my fingers. When he comes up he's put on his proper clothes. Long white shirt, sash and what not. Loincloth underneath. All spotless. Like Jesus. Only not. I watch him undress and think about them all at Evensong and Geoffrey praying in that pausy way he does, giving you time to mean each phrase. And the fan club lapping it up, thinking they love God when they just love Geoffrey. Lighten our darkness we beseech thee O Lord and by thy great mercy defend us from all perils and dangers of this night. Like Mr Ramesh who is twenty-six with lovely legs, who goes swimming every morning at Merrion Street Baths and plays hockey for Horsforth. I ask him if they offer their sex to God. He isn't very interested in the point but with them, so far as I can gather, sex is all part of God anyway. I can see why too. It's the first time I really understand what all the fuss is about. There among the lentils on the second Sunday after Trinity.

I've just popped into the vestry. He's put a lock on the cupboard door.

Go to black.

Come up on Susan sitting in the drawing-room of the vicarage. Much smarter than in previous scenes, she has had her hair done and seems a different woman. Evening.

I stand up and say, 'My name is Susan. I am a vicar's wife and I am an alcoholic.' Then I tell my story. Or some of it anyway. 'Don't pull any

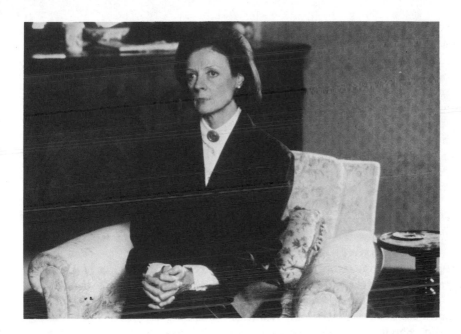

punches,' says Clem, my counsellor. 'Nobody's going to be shocked,
believe me love, we've all been there.' But I don't tell them about Mr
Ramesh because they've not been there. 'Listen, people. I was so drunk I
used to go and sleep with an Asian grocer. Yes, and you won't believe this.
I loved it. Loved every minute.' Dear oh dear. This was a real drunken
lady.

So I draw a veil over Mr Ramesh who once, on the feast of St Simon and
St Jude (Choral Evensong at six, daily services at the customary hour), put
make-up on his eyes and bells on his ankles, and naked except for his little
belt danced in the back room of the shop with a tambourine.

'So how did you come to AA?' they ask. 'My husband,' I say. 'The vicar.
He persuaded me.' But I lie. It was not my husband, it was Mr Ramesh,
the exquisitely delicate and polite Mr Ramesh who one Sunday night
turned his troubled face towards me with its struggling moustache and
asked if he might take the bull by the horns and enquire if intoxication was
a prerequisite for sexual intercourse, or whether it was only when I was
going to bed with him, the beautiful Mr Ramesh, twenty-six, with
wonderful legs, whether it was only with him I had to be inebriated. And

was it, asked this slim, flawless and troubled creature, was it perhaps his colour? Because if not he would like to float the suggestion that sober might be even nicer. So the credit for the road to Damascus goes to Mr Ramesh, whose first name turns out also to be Ramesh. Ramesh Ramesh, a member of the community council and the Leeds Federation of Trade.

But none of this I say. In fact I never say anything at all. Only when it becomes plain to Geoffrey (and it takes all of three weeks) that Mrs Vicar is finally on the wagon, who is it gets the credit? Not one of Mr Ramesh's jolly little gods, busy doing everything under the sun to one another, much like Mr Ramesh. Oh no. It's full marks to Geoffrey's chum, the Deity, moving in his well-known mysterious way.

So now everything has changed. For the moment I am a new woman and Geoffrey is a new man. And he brings it up on the slightest pretext. 'My wife's an alcoholic, you know. Yes. It's a great challenge to me and to the parish as extended family.' From being a fly in the ointment I find myself transformed into a feather in his cap. Included it in his sermon on Prayers Answered when he reveals that he and the fan club have been having these jolly get togethers in which they'd all prayed over what he calls 'my problem'. It practically sent me racing back to the Tio Pepe even to think of it. The fans, of course, never dreaming that their prayers would be answered, are furious. They think it's brought us closer together. Geoffrey thinks that too. We were at some doleful diocesan jamboree last week and I'm stuck there clutching my grapefruit juice as Geoffrey's telling the tale to some bearded cleric. Suddenly he seizes my hand. 'We met it with love,' he cries, as if love were some all-purpose antibiotic, which to Geoffrey it probably is.

And it goes on, the mileage in it endless. I said to Geoffrey that when I stood up at AA I sometimes told the story about the flower arranging. Result: he starts telling it all over the diocese. The first time was at a conference on The Supportive Parish. Gales of deep, liberated, caring laughter. He's now given it a new twist and tells the story as if he's talking about a parishioner, then at the end he says, 'Friends I want to tell you something. (Deep hush.) That drunken flower-arranger was my wife.' Silence . . . then the applause, *terrific*.

I've caught the other young, upwardly mobile parsons sneaking looks at me now and again and you can see them thinking why weren't they smart enough to marry an alcoholic or better still a drug addict, problem wives whom they could do a nice redemption job on, right there on their own doorstep. Because there's no stopping Geoffrey now. He grips my hand in public, nay *brandishes* it. 'We're a team,' he cries. Looks certain to be rural dean and that's only the beginning. As the bishop says, 'Just the kind of man we're looking for on the bench . . . someone with a seasoned compassion, someone who's looked life in the face. Someone who's been there.'

Mr Ramesh sold his shop. He's gone back to India to fetch his wife. She's old enough now apparently. I went down there on Sunday. There was a boy writing Under New Management on the window. Spelled wrong. And something underneath in Hindi, spelled right probably. He said he thought Mr Ramesh would be getting another shop, only in Preston.

They do that, of course, Asians, build something up, get it going nicely, then take the profit and move on. It's a good thing. We ought to be more like that, more enterprising.

My group meets twice a week and I go. Religiously. And that's what it is, of course. The names are different, Frankie and Steve, Susie and Clem. But it's actually Miss Frobisher and Mrs Shrubsole all over again. I never liked going to one church so I end up going to two. Geoffrey would call that the wonderful mystery of God. I call it bad taste. And I wouldn't do it to a dog. But that's the thing nobody ever says about God . . . he has no taste at all.

Fade out.

A Lady of Letters

IRENE RUDDOCK   Patricia Routledge

Produced by Innes Lloyd
Directed by Giles Foster
Designed by Tony Burrough
Music by George Fenton

Miss Ruddock is an ordinary middle-aged woman. The room in which we see her is simply furnished and there is a bay window. It is afternoon.

I can't say the service was up to scratch. It smacked of the conveyor-belt. In fact I wrote to the crematorium. I said I thought the hallmark of a ceremony of that nature was reverence, whereas the word that kept coming into my mind was brisk. Moreover, I added, grief-stricken people do not expect to emerge from the Chapel of Rest to find grown men skulking in the rhododendrons with tab-ends in their mouths. If the hearse drivers must smoke then facilities should be provided. I'd heard good reports of this crematorium, but I hoped that they would agree with me that on this occasion it had let itself down.

Of course if I'd happened to be heartbroken I'd have felt much worse. I didn't let on to the crematorium because I thought it might get them off the hook but I actually didn't know her all that well. I used to see her getting on the 37 and we'd pass the time of day. She lost her mother round about the time I lost mine, she had a niece in Australia and I have the one cousin in Canada, then she went in for gas-fired central heating just a few weeks before I did, so one way and another we covered a lot of the same ground. I'd spent years thinking she was called Hammersley, which was way off the mark because her name turns out to be Pringle. There was a picture of her in the *Evening Post* (she'd been a big voluntary worker) with details of the funeral on the Wednesday afternoon, which is the one time I'm dangling my feet a bit, so I thought I'd get out my little maroon coat and put in an appearance. At least it's an outing. And I was glad I'd gone but, as I say, the ceremony was a bit lack-lustre and topped off by these young fellers smoking, so I thought the least I could do was write.

Anyway I had a charming letter back from the director of operations, a Mr Widdop. He said he was most grateful I'd drawn this matter to his attention and, while he was aware the practice sometimes went on, if he personally caught anybody smoking he would jump on the culprits with both feet. He knew I would appreciate that discipline within the chapel precincts presented special problems as it wasn't always convenient to tear a strip off somebody when there were grief-stricken people knocking about. What he personally preferred to do was to keep a low profile, then come down on the offenders like a ton of bricks once the coast was clear. With regard to my remarks about facilities, they had no plans to provide a smoking area in the Chapel of Rest in the foreseeable future as I must

understand that space was at a premium and top of their list of priorities at
the present moment was the provision of a temporary temple for the use of
racial minorities. However, he would bear my remarks in mind, and if I
were to come across any similar infringements in the future I was not to
hesitate to get in touch.

I wrote him a little letter back thanking him for his prompt and
courteous reply and saying that though I hoped not to be making any
further visits to the crematorium in the near future (joke) I took his point.
I also dropped a line to the relatives, care of the undertakers, saying that I
was an acquaintance of Miss Pringle, had been present at the ceremony
and had taken the liberty of entering into correspondence with the
crematorium over the unfortunate lapse. I enclosed a copy of Mr Widdop's
reply but they didn't write back, which I can understand because the one
thing death always entails is a mass of correspondence. When Mother died
I had fifty-three letters. Besides, they may not have even seen them
smoking, they were probably blinded with grief. I see we've got a new
couple moved in opposite. Don't look very promising. The kiddy looks
filthy.

Go to black.

Come up on Miss Ruddock in the same setting. Morning.

A card from the opticians this morning saying that their records indicate
that it's two years since they supplied me with spectacles and that by now
they would almost certainly be in need of verification and suggesting I call
at my earliest convenience. I thought that was nice so I took my trusty
Platignum and dashed off an answer forthwith. I said I thought it was very
considerate of them to have kept me in mind and while I was quite satisfied
with my spectacles at the present moment I was grateful to them for
drawing the matter to my attention and in the event of my noticing any
deterioration I would in due course get in touch with them. (*She picks up
her pen.*) It's stood me in good stead has this pen. Mother bought it me the
last time she was able to get over to Harrogate. It's been a real friend. (*She
glances in the direction of the window.*)

Angie her name is. I heard him shout of her as I went by en route for the
Post Office. He was laid out underneath his car wanting a spanner and she
came out, transistor in one hand, kiddy in the other. Thin little thing,
bruise on its arm. I thought, 'Well, you've got a car, you've got a

transistor, it's about time you invested in some curtains.' She can't be more than twenty and by the look of her she's expecting another.

I passed the place where there was the broken step I wrote to the council was a danger to the public. Little ramp there now, access for the disabled. Whenever I pass I think, 'Well, that's thanks to you, Irene.' My monument that ramp. Only some dog had gone and done its business right in the middle of it. I'm sure there's more of that than there used to be. I had a little Awayday to London last year and it was dog dirt everywhere. I spotted some on the pavement right outside Buckingham Palace. I wrote to the Queen about it. Had a charming letter back from a lady in waiting saying that Her Majesty appreciated my interest and that my letter had been passed on to the appropriate authority. The upshot eventually is I get a long letter from the chief cleansing officer to Westminster City Council apologising profusely and enclosing a rundown of their Highways and Maintenance Budget. That's been my experience generally . . . people are only too grateful to have these things pointed out. The keynote is participation. Of course I wrote back to thank him and then blow me if I didn't get another letter thanking me for mine. So I wrote back saying I hadn't been expecting another letter and there was no need to have written again and was this an appropriate use of public resources? They didn't even bother to reply. Typical.

Pause.

I'm just waiting for the paper coming. Not that there's much in it. The correspondence I initiated on the length of the Archbishop of Canterbury's hair seems to have gone off the boil. Till I wrote up to Live Letters nobody'd actually spotted it. Various people took up the cudgels until there was an impassioned letter from the Rural Dean of Halifax who has a beard and that seems to have put the tin hat on it.

Getting dark.

The couple opposite just having their tea. No cloth on. They must have put the kiddy to bed. When I put the milk bottle out I heard it crying.

Go to black.

Come up on Miss Ruddock sitting in an easy chair reading the newspaper. Afternoon.

Prison, they have it easy. Television, table tennis, art. It's just a holiday camp, do you wonder there's crime? And people say, 'Well, what can you do?' Well, you can get on to your MP for a start. I do, regularly. Got a reply to one letter this morning. I'd written drawing his attention to a hitherto unnoticed factor in the rise in crime, namely the number of policemen these days who wear glasses. What chance would they have against a determined assailant? He noted my comments and promised to make them known in the proper quarter. He's Labour but it's always very good notepaper and beautifully typed.

When I'd dusted round and done my jobs I had a walk on to the end and bought a little packet of pork sausage and some Basildon Bond. Big black hair in the sausage. So I wrote off to the makers enclosing the hair. Stuck it under a bit of sellotape. Little arrow: 'This is the hair.' I emphasised that I didn't want a substitute packet, as it was plainly manufactured under unhygienic conditions, so would they send me a refund of the purchase price plus the cost of postage. I don't want inundating with sausage.

I keep wondering about the kiddy opposite. Haven't seen it for a week or two. And they're out all the time. Every single night they go off, and the kiddy doesn't go. And nobody comes in to sit. It can't be more than five. Where do they get the money to go out, that's what I'd like to know? Because he's not working. Spends all day tinkering with that car. There wants to be a bit less of the car and a bit more of the kiddy. It never plays out and they want fresh air do kiddies, it's a well-known fact. You don't hear it crying now, nothing. And I've never seen a cloth on. Teapot stuck there, Milk bottle. It'll surprise me if they're married. He has a tattoo anyway.

Go to black.

Come up on Miss Ruddock sitting on a dining chair in the window. Dusk.

My mother knew everybody in this street. She could reel off the occupants of every single house. Everybody could, once upon a time. Now, they come and they go. That's why these tragedies happen. Nobody watching. If they knew they were being watched they might behave. I'd talk to next door's about it only there hasn't been any contact since the business over the dustbins. And this other side's Asians so they won't know what's normal and what isn't. Though I've a feeling he's been educated and their kiddies are always beautifully turned out. I just wish they'd do something about their privet.

I thought I'd go and have a word with the doctor, drop a hint there somehow. There used to be just one doctor. Now they've all amalgamated so it's a bit of a lucky dip. Young fellow. I said I was getting upset, like I did before. 'Before what?' he said. I said, 'It's in my notes.' So he read them and then said, 'You've been getting a bit upset, like you did before. I'll give you something to take.' So I told him about the kiddy, and he said, 'Well, these tablets will help you to take a more balanced view.' I gave them three or four days and they didn't seem to me to make much difference so I went along again. Different doctor this time. Same rigmarole. I said I didn't want any more tablets, I just wanted the name of the firm manufacturing the ones I'd already had, because I think they ought to be told if their product isn't doing the trick. The doctor said it would be easier if he gave me some new tablets and anyway I couldn't write, the firm was Swiss. I said, 'What difference does that make, everybody speaks English now.' He said, 'We don't want to get into that, do we?' and writes me another prescription. I shan't bother with it. In fact I put it down the toilet. I don't know who you write to about doctors.

After I'd had my tea I sat in the front room in the dark watching the house. He's messing about with the car, one of those little vests on they have now without sleeves. Radio going hammer and tongs. No kiddy still. I don't even know their name.

Go to black.

Come up on Miss Ruddock in her hat and coat against a bare background.

Thinking about it afterwards, I realised it must have been the doctor that alerted the vicar. Came round anyway. Not the old vicar. I'd have known him. This was a young fellow in a collar and tie, could have been anybody. I didn't take the chain off. I said, 'How do I know you're the vicar, have you any identification?' He shoves a little cross round the door. I said, 'What's this?' He said, 'A cross.' I said, 'A cross doesn't mean anything. Youths wear crosses nowadays. Hooligans. They wear crosses in their ears.' He said, 'Not like this. This is a real cross. A working cross. It's the tool of my trade.' I was still a bit dubious, then I saw he had cycle clips on so I let him in.

He chats for a bit, this and that, no mention of God for long enough. They keep him up their sleeve for as long as they can, vicars, they know it puts people off. Went through a long rigmarole about love. How love comes in different forms . . . loving friends, loving the countryside, loving music. People would be surprised to learn, he said (and I thought, 'Here we go'), people would be surprised to learn that they loved God all the time and just didn't know it. I cut him short. I said, 'If you've come round here to talk about God you're barking up the wrong tree. I'm an atheist.' He was a bit stumped, I could see. They don't expect you to be an atheist when you're a miss. Vicars, they think if you're a single person they're on a good wicket. He said, 'Well, Miss Ruddock, I shall call again. I shall look on you as a challenge.'

He hadn't been gone long when there's another knock, only this time it's a policeman, with a woman policeman in tow. Ask if they can come in and have a word. I said, 'What for?' He said, 'You know what for.' I said, 'I don't,' but I let them in. Takes his helmet off, only young and says he'll come straight to the point: was it me who'd been writing these letters? I said, 'What letters? I don't write letters.' He said, 'Letters.' I said, 'Everyone writes letters. I bet you write letters.' He said, 'Not like you, love.' I said, 'Don't love me. You'd better give me your name and number. I intend to write to your superintendent.'

It turns out it's to do with the couple opposite. I said, 'Well, why are you asking me?' He said, 'We're asking you because who was it wrote to the chemist saying his wife was a prostitute? We're asking you because who was it gave the lollipop man a nervous breakdown?' I said, 'Well, he was interfering with those children.' He said, 'The court bound you over to keep the peace. This is a serious matter.' I said, 'It is a serious matter. I can't keep the peace when there's cruelty and neglect going on under my nose. I shouldn't keep the peace when there's a child suffering. It's not my duty to keep the peace then, is it?' So then madam takes over, the understanding approach. She said didn't I appreciate this was a caring young couple? I said if they were a caring young couple why did you never see the kiddy? If they were a caring young couple why did they go gadding off every night, leaving the kiddy alone in the house? She said because the kiddy wasn't alone in the house. The kiddy wasn't in the house. The kiddy was in hospital in Bradford, that's where they were going every night. And that's where the kiddy died, last Friday. I said, 'What of? Neglect?' She said, 'No. Leukaemia.'

Pause.

He said, 'You'd better get your hat and coat on.'

Go to black.

Come up on Miss Ruddock back at home. Day.

I've got two social workers come, one white, one black. Maureen I'm
supposed to call the white one, shocking finger nails, ginger hair, and last
week a hole in her tights as big as a 50p piece. She looks more in need of
social work than I do. Puts it all down to men. 'We all know about men,
don't we, Irene.' I never said she could call me Irene. I don't want to be
called Irene. I want to be called Miss Ruddock. I'm not Irene. I haven't
been Irene since Mother died. But they all call me Irene, her, the police,
everybody. They think they're being nice, only it's just a nice way of being
nasty. The other one's Asian, Mrs Rabindi, little red spot on her forehead,
all that. Sits, talks. She's right enough. Said I'd be useful in India. You
can earn a living writing letters there apparently as they're all illiterate.
Something daubed on her door last week. She says it's what you get to
expect if you're Asian. I said, 'Well, there's all sorts gets chucked over my
wall.' We sit and talk, only she's a bit of a boring woman. I tell her I loved
my mother and she says how she loved her mother. I tell her I'm
frightened to walk the streets and she tells me how she's been attacked
herself. Well, it doesn't get you any further. It's all 'me too'. Social work,
I think it's just chiming in.

I'm on what's called a suspended sentence. It means you have to toe the
line. If I write any more letters I get sent to prison. The magistrate said I
was more to be pitied than anything else. I said, 'Excuse me, could I
interject?' He said, 'No. Your best plan would be to keep mum.' Big
fellow, navy blue suit, poppy in his buttonhole. Looked a bit of a drinker.

Maureen says I should listen to local radio. Join these phone-in things.
Chat to the disc jockey and choose a record. She says they're very effective
in alleviating loneliness and a sense of being isolated in the community. I
said, 'Yes and they're even more effective in bumping up the phone bill.'
Maureen's trying to get me on reading. I suppose to get me off writing.
She says books would widen my horizon. Fetches me novels, but they
don't ring true. I mean, when somebody in a novel says something like
'I've never been in an air crash', you know this means that five minutes
later they will be. Say trains never crash and one does. In stories saying it
brings it on. So if you get the heroine saying, 'I don't suppose I shall ever
be happy', then you can bank on it there's happiness just around the
corner. That's the rule in novels. Whereas in life you can say you're never

going to be happy and you never are happy, and saying it doesn't make a ha'porth of difference. That's the real rule. Sometimes I catch myself thinking it'll be better the second time round. (*Pause.*) But this is it. This has been my go.

Pause.

New policeman now. Walks the streets, the way they used to. Part of the new policy. Community policing. Smiles. Passes the time of day. Keeping an eye on things.

Certainly keeps an eye on No. 56. In there an hour at a stretch. Timed it the other day and when eventually he comes out she's at the door in just a little shorty housecoat thing.

He's in there now.

Pause.

He wants reporting.

Go to black.

Come up on Miss Ruddock against a plain institutional background. She is in a tracksuit, speaks very quickly and is radiant.

I ought to be writing up my diary. Mrs Proctor's got us all on keeping diaries as part of Literary Appreciation. The other girls can't think what to put in theirs, me I can't think what to leave out. Trouble is I never have time to write it up, I'm three days behind as it is.

I'm that busy. In a morning it's Occupation and I've opted for bookbinding and dressmaking. In dressmaking Mrs Dunlop's chucked me in at the deep end and I'm running up a little cocktail dress. I said, 'I never have cocktails.' She said, 'Well, now you've got the dress, you can.' That's what it's geared to, this place, new horizons. It's in shantung with a little shawl collar. Lucille's making me a chunky necklace for it in Handicrafts.

I share a room with Bridget, who's from Glasgow. She's been a prostitute on and off and did away with her kiddy, accidentally, when she was drunk and upset. Bonny little face, you'd never think it. Her mother was blind, but made beautiful pastry and brought up a family of nine in three rooms. You don't know you're born I think. I'm friends with practically everyone though besides Bridget. I'm up and down this

corridor; more often than not I'm still on my rounds when the bell goes.

They laugh at me, I know, but it's all in good part. Lucille says, 'You're funny you, Irene. You don't mind being in prison.' I said, 'Prison!' I said, 'Lucille. This is the first taste of freedom I've had in years.'

Of course I'm lucky. The others miss the sex. Men, men, men. They talk about nothing else.

Mind you, that's not quite the closed book it used to be. Bridget's taken me through the procedure step by step and whereas previous to this if I'd ever found myself in bed with a man I should have been like a fish out of water, now, as Bridget says, at least I know the rudiments. Of course I can't ever see it coming to that at my age, but still it's nice to have another string to your bow. They've got me smoking now and again as well. I mean, I shan't ever be a full-time smoker, I'm not that type, and I don't want to be, but it means that if I'm ever in a social situation when I'm called on to smoke, like when they're toasting the Queen, I shan't be put off my stroke. But you see, that's the whole philosophy of this place: acquiring skills.

I sailed through the secretarial course, Miss Macaulay says I'm their first Grade I. I can type like the wind. Miss Macaulay says we mustn't let the grass grow under our feet and if she goes down on her knees in Admin they might (repeat might) let me have a go on their word processor. Then the plan is: Stage One, I go on day release for a bit, followed by Stage Two a spell in a resettlement hostel where I'll be reintegrated into the community. Then finally Stage Three a little job in an office somewhere. I said to Miss Macaulay, 'Will it matter my having been in prison?' She said, 'Irene, with your qualifications it wouldn't matter if you'd been in the SS.'

But the stuff some of them come out with! You have to smile. They have words for things I didn't know there were words for, and in fact I swear myself on occasion now, though only when the need arises. The other evening I'm sat with Shirley during Association. Shirley's very obese, I think it's glandular, and we're trying to put together a letter to her boy friend. Well, she says it's her boy friend only I had to start the letter three times because first go off she says his name's Kenneth, then she says it's Mark, and finally she settles on Stephen. She stammers does Shirley and I think she just wanted a name she could say. I don't believe she has a boy friend at all, just wants to be in the swim. She shouldn't actually be in here in fact, she's not all there but there's nowhere else to put her apparently, she sets fire to places. Anyway, we're sitting in her room concocting this letter to her pretend boy friend when Black Geraldine waltzes in and drapes herself across the bed and starts chipping in, saying was this boy friend blond, did he have curly hair, and then nasty personal-type questions she should know better than to ask Shirley. And Shirley's getting confused and stammering and Geraldine's laughing, so finally I threw caution to the winds and told Geraldine to fuck up.

She screams with laughing and goes running down the corridor saying, 'Do you know what Irene said, do you know what Irene said?' When she'd gone Shirley said, 'You shouldn't have said that.' I said, 'I know, but sometimes it's necessary.' She said, 'No, Irene. I don't mean you shouldn't have said it. Only you got it wrong. It's not fuck up.' I said, 'What is it?' She said, 'It's fuck off.' She's good-hearted.

Pause.

Sometimes Bridget will wake up in the middle of the night shouting, dreaming about the kiddy she killed, and I go over and sit by the bed and hold her hand till she's gone off again. There's my little clock ticking and I can hear the wind in the poplar trees by the playing field and maybe it's raining and I'm sitting there. And I'm so *happy*.

Fade out.

Her Big Chance

LESLEY   Julie Walters

Produced by Innes Lloyd
Directed by Giles Foster
Designed by Tony Burrough
Music by George Fenton

Lesley is in her early thirties. She is in her flat. Morning.

I shot a man last week. In the back. I miss it now, it was really interesting. Still, I'm not going to get depressed about it. You have to look to the future. To have something like that under your belt can be quite useful, you never know when you might be called on to repeat the experience.

It wasn't in the line of duty. I wasn't a policewoman or someone who takes violence in their stride. It was with a harpoon gun actually, but it definitely wasn't an accident. My decision to kill was arrived at only after a visible tussle with my conscience. I had to make it plain that once I'd pulled the trigger things were never going to be the same again: this was a woman at the crossroads.

It wasn't Crossroads, of course. They don't shoot people in Crossroads, at any rate not with harpoon guns. If anybody did get shot it would be with a weapon more suited to the motel ambience. I have been in Crossroads though, actually. I was in an episode involving a fork lunch. At least I was told it was a fork lunch, the script said it was a finger buffet. I said to the floor manager, I said, 'Rex. Are you on cans because I'd like some direction on this point. Are we toying or are we tucking in?' He said, 'Forget it. We're losing the food anyway.' I was playing Woman in a Musquash Coat, a guest at a wedding reception, and I was scheduled just to be in that one episode. However in my performance I tried to suggest I'd taken a fancy to the hotel in the hope I might catch the director's eye and he'd have me stay on after the fork lunch for the following episode which involved a full-blown weekend. So I acted an interest in the soft furnishings, running my fingers over the formica and admiring the carpet on the walls. Only Rex came over to say that they'd put me in a musquash coat to suggest I was a sophisticated woman, could I try and look as if I was more at home in a three star motel. I wasn't at home in that sort of motel I can tell you. I said to the man I'd been put next to, who I took to be my husband, I said, 'Curtains in orange nylon and no place mats, there's not even the veneer of civilisation.' He said, 'Don't talk to me about orange nylon. I was on a jury once that sentenced Richard Attenborough to death.' We'd been told to indulge in simulated cocktail chit-chat so we weren't being unprofessional, talking. That is something I pride myself on, actually: I am professional to my fingertips.

Whatever it is I'm doing, even if it's just a walk-on, I must must must get involved, right up to the hilt. I can't help it. People who know me tell

me I'm a very serious person, only it's funny, I never get to do serious
parts. The parts I get offered tend to be fun-loving girls who take life as it
comes and aren't afraid of a good time should the opportunity
arise-type-thing. I'd call them vivacious if that didn't carry overtones of
the outdoor life. In a nutshell I play the kind of girl who's very much at
home on a bar stool and who seldom has to light her own cigarette. That
couldn't be more different from me because for a start I'm not a smoker. I
mean, I can smoke if a part requires it. I'm a professional and you need as
many strings to your bow as you can in this game. But, having said that,
I'm not a natural smoker and what's more I surprise my friends by not
being much of a party-goer either. (Rather curl up with a book quite
frankly.) *However*, this particular party I'd made an exception. Thing was
I'd met this ex-graphic designer who was quitting the rat race and going
off to Zimbabwe and he was having a little farewell do in the flat of an air
hostess friend of his in Mitcham, would I go? I thought, well it's not every
day you get somebody going off to Zimbabwe, so I said 'Yes' and I'm glad
I did because that's how I got the audition.

Now my hobby is people. I collect people. So when I saw this
interesting-looking man in the corner, next thing is I find myself talking to
him. I said, 'You look an interesting person. I'm interested in interesting
people. Hello.' He said, 'Hello.' I said, 'What do you do?' He said, 'I'm
in films.' I said, 'Oh, that's interesting, anything in the pipeline?' He said,
'As a matter of fact, yes,' and starts telling me about this project he's
involved in making videos for the overseas market, targeted chiefly on
West Germany. I said, 'Are you the producer?' He said, 'No, but I'm on
the production side, the name's Spud.' I said, 'Spud! That's an interesting
name, mine's Lesley.' He said, 'As it happens, Lesley, we've got a problem
at the moment. Our main girl has had to drop out because her back's
packed in. Are you an actress?' I said, 'Well, Spud, interesting that you
should ask because as a matter of fact I am.' He said, 'Will you excuse me
one moment, Lesley?' I said, 'Why, Spud, where are you going?' He said,
'I'm going to go away, Lesley, and make one phone call.'

It transpires the director is seeing possible replacements the very next
day, at an address in West London. Spud said, 'It's interesting because
I'm based in Ealing.' I said, 'Isn't that West London?' He said, 'It is.
Where's your stamping ground?' I said, 'Bromley, for my sins.' He said,
'That's a far-ish cry. Why not bed down at my place?' I said, 'Thank you,
kind sir, but I didn't fall off the Christmas tree yesterday.' He said,

'Lesley, I have a son studying hotel management and a daughter with one kidney. Besides, I've got my sister-in-law staying. She's come up for the Ideal Home Exhibition.'

The penny began to drop when I saw the tattoo. My experience of tattoos is that they're generally confined to the lower echelons, and when I saw his vest it had electrician written all over it. I never even saw the sister-in-law. Still traipsing round Olympia probably.

Go to black.

Come up on Lesley in the same setting. Afternoon.

I know something about personality. There's a chapter about it in this book I'm reading. It's by an American. They're the experts where personality is concerned, the Americans; they've got it down to a fine art. It makes a big thing of interviews so I was able to test it out.

The director's not very old, blue suit, tie loose, sleeves turned back. I put him down as a university type. Said his name was Simon, which I instantly committed to memory. (That's one of the points in the book: purpose and use of name.) He said, 'Forgive this crazy time.' I said, 'I'm sorry, Simon?' He said, 'Like 9.30 in the morning.' I said, 'Simon. The day begins when the day begins. You're the director.' He said, 'Yes, well. Can you tell me what you've done?'

I said, 'Where you may have seen me, Simon, is in *Tess*. Roman Polanski. I played Chloë.' 'I don't remember her,' he said. 'Is she in the book?' I said, 'Book? This is *Tess*, Simon. Roman Polanski. Chloë was the one on the back of the farm cart wearing a shawl. The shawl was original nineteenth-century embroidery. All hand done. Do you know Roman, Simon?' He said, 'Not personally, no.' I said, 'Physically he's quite small but we had a very good working relationship. Very open.' He said that was good, because Travis in the film was very open. I said, 'Travis? That's an interesting name, Simon.' He said, 'Yes. She's an interesting character, she spends most of the film on the deck of a yacht.' I said, 'Yacht? That's interesting, Simon. My brother-in-law has a small power boat berthed at Ipswich.' He said, 'Well! Snap!' I said, 'Yes, small world!' He said, 'In an ideal world, Lesley, I'd be happy to sit here chatting all day but I have a pretty tight schedule and, although I know it's only 9.30 in the morning, could I see you in your bra and panties?' I said, '9.30 in the morning, 10.30 at night, we're both professionals, Simon, but', I said, 'could we

just put another bar on because if we don't you won't be able to tell my tits from goose-pimples.' He had to smile. That was another of the sections in the personality book: humour, usefulness of in breaking the ice.

When I'd got my things off he said, 'Well, you've passed the physical. Now the oral. Do you play chess?' I said, 'Chess, Simon? Do you mean the musical?' He said, 'No, the game.' I said, 'As a matter of fact, Simon, I don't. Is that a problem?' He said, 'Not if you water-ski. Travis is fundamentally an outdoor girl, but we thought it might be fun to make her an intellectual on the side.' I said, 'Well, Simon, I'm very happy to learn both chess and water-skiing, but could I make a suggestion? Reading generally indicates a studious temperament and I'm a very convincing reader,' I said, 'because it's something I frequently do in real life.' I could tell he was impressed. And so I said, 'Another suggestion I could make would be to kit Travis out with some glasses. Spectacles, Simon. These days they're not unbecoming and if you put Travis in spectacles with something in paperback, that says it all.' He said, 'You've been most helpful.' I said, 'The paperback could be something about the environment or, if you want to maintain the water-skiing theme, something about water-skiing and the environment possibly. I mean, Lake Windermere.'

He was showing me out by this time but I said, 'One last thought, Simon, and that is a briefcase. Put Travis in a bikini and give her a briefcase and you get the best of every possible world.' He said, 'I'm most grateful. You've given me a lot of ideas.' I said, 'Goodbye, Simon. I hope we can work together.' The drill for saying goodbye is you take the person's hand and then put your other hand over theirs, clasp it warmly while at the same time looking into their eyes, smiling and reiterating their name. This lodges you in their mind apparently. So I did all that, only going downstairs I had another thought and I popped back. He was on the phone. 'You won't believe this,' he was saying. I said, 'Don't hang up, Simon, only I just wanted to make it crystal clear that when I said briefcase I didn't mean the old-fashioned type ones, there are new briefcases now that open up and turn into a mini writing-desk. Being an up-to-the-minute girl, that would probably be the kind of briefcase Travis would have. She could be sitting in a wet bikini with a briefcase open on her knee. I've never seen that on screen so it would be some kind of first. Ciao, Simon. Take care.'

Pause.

That was last Friday. The book's got charts where you check your interview score. Mine was 75. Very good to excellent. Actually, I'm surprised they haven't telephoned.

Go to black.

Come up on Lesley, who is now made up and her hair done, sitting in a small bleak room in her dressing-gown. Morning.

You'd never think this frock wasn't made for me. I said to Scott, who's Wardrobe, 'She must be my double.' He said, 'No. You're hers. The stupid cow.'

Talk about last-minute, though. Eleven o'clock on Tuesday night I'm just wondering about having a run round with the dustette, six o'clock next morning I'm sitting in Lee-on-Solent in make-up. When the phone went telling me I'd got the part I assumed it was Simon. So I said, 'Hello Simon.' He said, 'Try Nigel.' So I said, 'Well, Nigel, can you tell Simon that I haven't let the grass grow under my feet. I now play a rudimentary game of chess.' He said, 'I don't care if you play a championship game of ice hockey, just don't get pregnant.'

It transpires the girl they'd slated to do the part had been living with a racing driver and of course the inevitable happened, kiddy on the way. So my name was next out of the hat. I said to Scott, 'I know why. They knew I had ideas about the part.' He said, 'They knew you had a 38-inch bust.' His mother's confined to a wheelchair, he's got a lot on his plate.

Anyway, I'm ready. I've been ready since yesterday morning. It was long enough before anybody came near. I had a bacon sandwich which Scott went and fetched for me while I was under the dryer. I said, 'Wasn't there a croissant?' He said, 'In Lee-on-Solent?' On *Tess* there were croissants. On *Tess* there was filter coffee. There was also some liaison.

I wanted to talk to somebody about the part, only Scott said they were out in the speed boat doing mute shots of the coastline. On *Tess* you were never sitting around. Roman anticipated every eventuality. We filmed in the middle of a forest once and the toilet arrangements were immaculate. There was also provision for a calorie-controlled diet. I said to Scott, 'I'm not used to working like this.' He said, 'Let's face it, dear. You're not used to working. Why didn't you bring your knitting?' I said, 'I do not knit, Scott.' He said, 'Well, file your nails then, pluck an eyebrow, be like me, do something constructive.' He's as thin as a rail and apparently an accomplished pianist and he seems to be make-up as well as wardrobe. On *Tess* we had three caravans for make-up alone.

Eventually Simon puts his head round the door. I said, 'Hello, Simon.' I said, 'Long time no see. Did Nigel tell you I've learned chess?' He said, 'Chess? Aren't you the one who can water-ski?' I said 'No.' He said 'Bugger' and disappeared. I said to Scott, 'Simon's on the young side for a director.' He said, 'Director? He couldn't direct you to the end of the street. He just does all the running about.' I said, 'Who is the director?' He said, 'Gunther.' I said, 'Gunther? That sounds a continental name.' He said, 'Yes. German.' I said, 'That's interesting. I went to Germany once. Dusseldorf.' He said, 'Well, you'll have a lot to talk about.' I've a feeling Scott may be gay. I normally like them only I think he's one of the ones it's turned bitter.

I'm still sitting there hours later when this other young fellow comes in. I said, 'Gunther?' He said, 'Nigel.' I said, 'We spoke on the phone.' He said, 'Yes. I'm about to commit suicide. I've just been told. You don't water-ski.' I said, 'Nigel. I could learn. I picked up the skateboard in five minutes.' He said, 'Precious. Five minutes is what we do not have. You don't by any chance have fluent French?' I said, 'No, why?' He said, 'They'd wondered about making her French.' I said, 'Nigel. How can she be French when she's called Travis? Travis isn't a French name.' He said, 'The name isn't important.' I said, 'It is to me. It's all I've got to build on.' He said, 'I'll get back to you.' I said, 'Nigel. I don't have French but what I do have is a smattering of Spanish, the legacy of several non-package type holidays on the Costa del Sol. Could Travis be half Spanish?' He said to Scott, 'We wanted someone with fluent French who could water-ski. What have we got? Someone with pidgin Spanish who plays chess.' Scott said, 'Well, don't tell me. I started off a landscape gardener.'

I was still waiting to be used in the afternoon which is when they did the water-skiing. Some girl from the local sub-aqua did it. She works part-time in the quayside restaurant where they all ate last night apparently. I saw her when she came in for make-up. Pleasant enough but didn't look a bit like me. I'm quite petite, only she was on the large side and whereas my hair is auburn hers was definitely ginger. I didn't say anything at the time but I thought if she's supposed to be me they'll be into big continuity problems so I thought I'd go in quest of the director and tell him. Nobody about on the yacht except a man who's dusting the camera. He said not to worry, the shot was p.o.v. water-skis so we'd only be seeing her elbow. I said, 'Will that work?' He said, 'Oh yes. You know, Cinema, the magic of.' Mind you, he said, if it was up to him personally, he'd rather see my elbow than hers any day. His name was Terry, what was mine? I said, 'It's a relief to find someone civil.' He said, 'It's the usual story, Lesley, Art comes in at the door, manners go out of the window. Why is making a film like being a mushroom?'

I said, 'Why, Terry?' He said, 'They keep you in the dark and every now and again somebody comes and throws a bucket of shit over you.' He laughed. I said, 'That's interesting, only Terry, they don't grow mushrooms like that now. It's all industrialised.' He said, 'You sound like a cultured person, what say we spend the evening exploring the delights of Lee-on-Solent?'

His room's nicer than mine. His bathroom's got a hair-dryer.

Go to black.

Come up on Lesley now in a bikini and wrap. An anonymous hotel room.
Evening.

Please don't misunderstand me. I've no objection to taking my top off. But
Travis as I was playing her wasn't the kind of girl who would take her top
off. I said, 'I'm a professional, Nigel. Credit me with a little experience. It
isn't Travis.'

I'd been sitting on the deck of the yacht all day as background while
these two older men had what I presumed was a business discussion. One
of them, who was covered in hair and had a real weight problem, was my
boyfriend apparently. You knew he was my boyfriend because at an earlier
juncture you'd seen him hit me across the face. Travis is supposed to be a
good-time girl, though you never actually see me having a good time, just
sat on this freezing cold deck plastering on the sun tan lotion. I said to
Nigel, 'I don't know whether the cameraman's spotted it, Nigel, but
would I be sunbathing? There's no sun.' Nigel said, 'No sun is favourite.'
Nigel's first assistant, here there and everywhere. Gunther never speaks,
not to me anyway. Just stands behind the camera with a little cap on. Not a
patch on Roman. Roman had a smile for everybody.

Anyway, I'm sitting there as background and I say to Nigel, 'Nigel, am
I right in thinking I'm a denizen of the cocktail belt?' He said, 'Why?' a
bit guardedly. I said, 'Because to me, Nigel, that implies a cigarette-
holder,' and I produced quite a modest one I happened to have brought
with me. He went and spoke to Gunther, only Gunther ruled there was to
be no smoking. I said, 'On grounds of health?' Nigel said, 'No. On
grounds of it making continuity a bugger.' I'd also brought a paperback
with me just to make it easier for props (which seemed to be Scott again).
Only I'd hardly got it open when Nigel relieved me of it and said they were
going for the sun tan lotion. I said, 'Nigel, I don't think the two are
incompatible. I can apply sun tan lotion and read at the same time. That is
what professionalism means.' He checked with Gunther again and he came
back and said, 'Forget the book. Sun tan lotion is favourite.' I said, 'Can I
ask you something else?' He said, 'Go on.' I said, 'What is my boyfriend
discussing?' He said, 'Business.' I said, 'Nigel. Would I be right in
thinking it's a drugs deal?' He said, 'Does it matter?' I said, 'It matters to
me. It matters to Travis. It helps my character.' He said, 'What would
help your character is if you took your bikini top off.' I said, 'Nigel.
Would Travis do that?' I said, 'We know Travis plays chess. She also

reads. Is Travis the type to go topless?' He said, 'Listen. Who do you think you're playing, Emily Brontë? Gunther wants to see your knockers.'

I didn't even look at him. I just took my top off without a word and applied sun tan lotion with all the contempt I could muster. They did the shot, then Nigel came over and said Gunther liked that and if I could give him a whisker more sensuality it might be worth a close-up. So we did it again and then Nigel came over and said Gunther was liking what I was giving them and in this next shot would I slip off my bikini bottom. I said, 'Nigel. Trust me. Travis would not do that.' Talks to Gunther. Comes back. Says Gunther agrees with me. The real Travis wouldn't. But by displaying herself naked before her boyfriend's business associate she is showing her contempt for his whole way of life. I said, 'Nigel. At last Gunther is giving me something I can relate to.' He says, 'Right! Let's shoot it! Elbow the bikini bottom!'

Pause.

We wrapped about six (that's film parlance for packed up). I said to Nigel, 'Did I give Gunther what he wanted? Is he happy?' He said, 'Gunther is an artist, Lesley. He's never happy. But as he said this afternoon, "At last we're cooking with gas." ' I said, 'Does that mean it's good?' He said, 'Yes.' I said, 'Oh. Because I prefer electricity.'

When I got back to the hotel, it took me some time to unwind. I'd become so identified with Travis it was only when I'd had a bath and freshened up I felt her loosening her hold on me. I was looking forward to relaxing with the crew, swapping anecdotes of the day's shooting in the knowledge of a day's work well done only when I got downstairs there was nobody about, just Scott and one of the drivers. Turns out all the rest of them had gone off to supper at the restaurant run by the fat girl who did the water-skiing.

I sat in the bar for a bit. Just one fellow in there. I said, 'My hobby is people, what do you do?' Lo and behold he's on the film too, the animal handler, Kenny. In charge of the cat. I said, 'That's interesting, Kenny. I didn't know there was going to be a cat. I love cats. I love dogs too, but I love cats.' He said, 'Would you care to see her? She's asleep on my bed.' I said, 'That's convenient.' He said, 'Lesley. Don't run away with that idea. I am wedded to my small charges.' So I go up and pal on with the cat a bit and Kenny tells me about all the animals he's handled, a zebra once, a seal, an alligator and umpteen ferrets. He has a trout there too in a tank. It was going to be caught later on in the film. Quite small, only they were going to shoot it in close-up so it would look bigger.

I sat on the bed and listened to him talk about animal behaviour. I said, 'Kenny, this is the kind of evening I like, two people just talking about something interesting.'

I woke up in the night and couldn't remember where I was. Then I saw the cat sitting there, watching the trout.

Go to black.

Come up on Lesley back in her own flat and in her ordinary clothes. Dusk.

When you've finished a shot on a film you have to wait and see whether there's what they call a hair in the gate. It's film parlance for the all clear. Thank God there wasn't because I couldn't have done it again. I'd created Travis and though it was her lover that got shot I felt it was the something in me that was Travis that had died.

My lover's name turned out to be Alfredo. That was my big line. 'Alfredo!' He was the head of some sort of crime syndicate only everybody in the yachting fraternity thought he was very respectable and to do with the building trade. One night while Alfredo and me were ashore at a building federation dinner and dance this young undercover policeman swims out to the yacht to search it in his underpants. However, as luck would have it Travis has a headache, so she and Alfredo return early from this ultra-respectable function with Alfredo in a towering rage. Originally I was down to say, 'I can't help it, Alfredo, I have a headache,' and we tried it once or twice only Gunther then thought it would be more convincing if my headache was so bad I couldn't actually speak and Alfredo just said, 'You and your headaches.' I said, 'If it's a migraine rather than a headache Travis probably wouldn't be able to speak,' and Gunther said, 'Whatever you say.' It's wonderful, that moment, when you feel a director first begin to trust you and you can really start to build.

Anyway Travis and Alfredo come into the cabin where they find this young man behind the sofa in his underpants and Alfredo takes out his gun and says, 'How lucky lovely Travis had a headache and we had to leave our glittering reception. I was cross with her then but now my mood has changed. Offer the gentleman a drink, Travis. Then go and take your clothes off. There's nothing I like better than making love after killing a policeman. Ha ha.' I then retire to the next cabin while Alfredo taunts this bare young policeman and says he is going to kill him, but before he does so, he tells him about his drug-smuggling operation in every detail, the way criminals tend to do the minute they get somebody at gunpoint. When Travis comes back with no clothes on the young policeman is talking about the evil drugs do, all the young lives ruined and so on. Only I forgot to say that there'd been some dialogue earlier, when I was supposed to be snorkelling, about how Travis had a little brother, Craig, and how he'd got hooked on drugs and how I was heartbroken and determined to revenge myself on the culprits should I ever come across them.

So when the policeman is saying all this about the horror of drugs you can see it comes as a revelation to Travis that her lover is involved in drugs: she thinks it's just been ordinary crime and stealing electrical goods. Anyway very quietly, 'almost pensively' Gunther said, Travis picks up an underwater spear gun that happens to be on the sideboard. Nigel came over and said that ideally at this point Gunther would like to see a variety of emotions chase themselves across Travis's face as her affection for her lover, Alfredo, fights with the demands of her conscience and the memories of her little brother, Craig. You see my lover's fat finger tighten on the trigger as he gets ready to shoot the policeman, only just then I say his name very quietly, 'Alfredo'. He spins round. Travis fires the harpoon and you see the spear come out of his back, killing him, and also ruining his dinner jacket. They then follow that with a big close-up with blood and everything, and me with a single tear rolling down my cheek.

We did this in one take, which Nigel said was almost unique in the annals of filming. Only Scott has to chip in and say good job, as just having one dinner jacket was fairly unique as well. I couldn't have done it again anyway. I'd got nothing left. Except I suddenly had a flash of inspiration, the way you do when you've been to the end of the world and back, and I said to Nigel, 'Don't you think that Travis, drained of all emotion by the death of her lover, would perhaps cling on to the policeman whose life she has saved, and that they would celebrate his deliverance by having sexual intercourse there and then?'

Big debate. Gunther really liked it, only the actor playing the policeman wasn't keen. I think he may have been gay too, he had a moustache. Eventually Nigel came over and said that favourite was for the policeman to look as if he was considering having sexual intercourse and for him to run his hand speculatively over Travis's private parts, only then pity drives out lust and instead he covers up her nakedness with an oriental-type dressing-gown, the property of her dead lover. Though even at this late stage you can tell he's not ruled out the possibility because as he's fastening the dressing-gown his fingers linger over Travis's nipples. Afterwards Gunther explained that if there had been any proper funny business at this point it would have detracted from the final scene when after all the excitement the undercover policeman goes home to his regular girlfriend, who cooks him a hot snack and who's a librarian, and then the final scene is of them making love, the message being that sexual intercourse is better with someone you're in love with even though they are a bit homely and work in the county library than with someone like Travis who's just after a good time. As Gunther said to me that night, 'It's a very moral film only the tragedy is, people won't see it.' I said to him, I said, 'That's interesting because I saw it that way right from the start.'

When we were in bed I said, 'If only we could have done this before.' He said, 'Lesley. I make it a rule never to lay a finger on an actress until the whole thing's in the can.' I said, 'Gunther. There's no need to explain. We're both professionals. But Gunther,' I said, 'can I ask you one question? Was I Travis? Were you pleased with my performance?' He said, 'Listen. If someone is a bad actress I can't sleep with her. So don't ask me if I was pleased with your performance. This is the proof.' He's a real artist is Gunther.

When I woke up in the morning he'd gone. I wandered down for some coffee only there was nobody from the unit about. I'd planned to say goodbye to everybody but they were off doing some establishing shots of the marina. Anyway, I went and bought a card with a sinking ship on it and put 'Goodbye, gang! See you at the première!' and left it at the desk.

As I came out with my bags Scott was just loading the laundry. I said, 'Ciao, Scott. It's been a pleasure working with you.' He said, 'You win some, you lose some.' I said, 'Now it's back to real life.' He said, 'Some of us never left it.' It's funny the way their clothes are always too small.

The film's coming out in West Germany initially, then Turkey possibly. Gunther says it'll make me quite famous. Well, I suppose I shall have to live with that. Only I'm not just going to sit here and wait for the phone to ring. No fear. I'm going to acquire another skill. Spoken Italian. Selling valuable oil paintings. Canoeing. You see, the more you have to offer as a person the better you are as an actress. Acting is really just giving.

Fade.

Soldiering On

MURIEL   Stephanie Cole

Produced by Innes Lloyd
Directed by Tristram Powell
Designed by Tony Burrough
Music by George Fenton

Muriel is a brisk, sensible woman in her late fifties. She is in a tweed skirt and cardigan with a single row of pearls, and we come on her settled in a corner of her comfortable home. It is afternoon.

It's a funny time, three o'clock, too late for lunch but a bit early for tea. Besides, there were one or two brave souls who'd trekked all the way from Wolverhampton; I couldn't risk giving them tea or we'd have had a mutiny on our hands. And I think people like to be offered something even if they don't actually eat it. One's first instinct was to make a beeline for the freezer and rout out the inevitable quiche, but I thought, 'Muriel, old girl, that's the coward's way out,' so the upshot was I stopped up till two in the morning trundling out a selection of my old standards . . . chicken in a lemon sauce, beef en croute from the old Colchester days (I thought of Jessie Marchant), and bushels of assorted salads. As it happened it wasn't exactly a salady day, quite crisp for April actually, however Mabel warmed up the proceedings with one of her famous soups, conjured up out of thin air, so we lived to fight another day. Nobody could quite put their finger on the flavour, so I was able to go round saying, 'Have you guessed the soup yet?' and that broke the ice a bit. I don't know what had got into Mabel but she'd gone mad and added a pinch of curry and that foxed most people. It was cauliflower actually.

 Still, it was a bit sticky at the start as these occasions generally are. There were people there one didn't know from Adam (all the Massey-Ferguson people for instance, completely unknown quantities to me), and then lots of people I knew I should know and didn't. But whenever I saw anyone looking lost I thought of Ralph and grabbed hold of someone I did know and breezed up saying, 'This is Jocelyn. She's at the Royal College of Art. I don't know your name but the odds are you're in agricultural machinery,' and then left them to it. It was a case of light the blue touch paper and retire.

 Knowing Ralph, of course, it was a real mixed bag. Several there from the Sports Council and quite a contingent from Tonbridge, some Friends of Norwich Cathedral and the Discharged Prisoners Aid Society, Madge and Perce whom we met on the *Mauretania* on our honeymoon, Donald and Joyce Bannerman who were actually en route for Abu Dhabi, then Donald bought a paper at Heathrow, saw the announcement and came straight down. And one sweet old man who'd come all the way over from Margate. He said, 'You won't remember me, Mrs Carpenter, but I'm a member of the criminal fraternity.' I shrieked. As the vicar said: Ralph touched life at many points.

The children magnificent, of course, or Giles at any rate. Luckily Margaret didn't appear. But Giles took off all the Household Brigade people on a tour of the garden while Pippa coped with some of the bigwigs from the City. 'I don't think you know George,' I heard one of them say, 'George cracks the whip at Goodison, Brown.' Poor souls, they both of them deserved medals. And Crispin and Lucy angelic, Crispin popping in and out of people's legs reaching up to fill the glasses. I wanted them to have a rest. 'No,' said Giles, 'let them do it. They adored their grandpa.' 'Adored him,' said Pippa, 'like we all did.'

The church had been absolutely chocker and I'd managed not to blub until right at the finish when they struck up with 'I vow to thee my country'. And then I'd a hundred and one things to do so I was perfectly all right until I saw awful Angela Gillespie had made the mistake of talking to boring old Frank from the firm, and I heard the dreaded words 'fork-lift trucks' and thought how many times I used to have to shut Ralph up in similar circumstances, and the idea of shutting Ralph up at all set me off instantly and I had to nip into the pantry to staunch the flow, shortly to be followed by Mabel who'd just fallen over one of his old wellingtons and promptly gone into floods. So we had a good laugh and a good cry over that before powdering our noses and hurling ourselves back into the fray.

When everybody'd gone I'm just having five minutes in the chair before tackling the debris when Margaret comes plunging into the room. She said, 'What were all those people?' I said, 'It was a kind of party for Daddy.' She said, 'Why? Is he dead?' I said, 'You know he's dead.' She said, 'Who killed him?' I said, 'Don't be such a donkey. Come along and we'll find you a tablet.' Some of Ralph's medicine's still in the cupboard. Fat lot of good that did, I thought, and poured it down the lav. Then felt a bit choked.

Anyway the tablet did the trick. I heard her walking about at two in the morning but I didn't get up. Except then I had to get up anyway because it suddenly came to me, in all the excitement I'd completely forgotten to feed the dogs.

Go to black.

Come up on Muriel sitting in an armchair. Evening.

Everybody I run into says not to take any big decisions. I staggered into the Community Centre bearing Ralph's entire wardrobe which Angela Gillespie had nipped in smartish and earmarked for Muscular Dystrophy. Five minutes later, Brenda Bousfield had come knocking at the door on behalf of Cystic Fibrosis. Knives out straightaway, I practically had to separate them. In fact I did separate them in the end, the City suits to Angela and Brenda the tweeds. All lovely stuff. Beautiful dinner jacket from Hawes and Curtis, done for Giles if he hadn't got so fat. Mind you, he didn't want the ties either. Angela did. 'Lovely jumble,' she said. 'How're you coping? Don't take any big decisions, one day at a time, I don't see any shoes.'

Actually I'd been silly and kept his shoes back. I loved his shoes. Always used to clean them. 'My shoeshine lady.' 'Whatever you do,' Angela said, 'don't give them to Brenda. They're top-heavy on staff, their group, it's well known. It all goes on the admin. We can use shoes.'

I thought I'd go into the library and see if Miss Dunsmore could find me something on bereavement. That's something I learned from Ralph: plug into other people's experience, pool your resources. 'A new experience is like travelling through unknown country. But remember, others have taken this road before you, old girl, and left notes. So Question no. 1: Is there a map? Question no. 2: Am I taking advantage of all the information available? It doesn't matter if you're going to get married, commit a burglary or keep a guinea pig; efficiency is the proper collation of information.' Oh Ralph.

Miss Dunsmore did a reconnoitre round, but the only information she could come up with was a book about burial customs in Papua New Guinea. I think even Ralph would draw the line at that. However, she thought the Health Centre did a pamphlet on bereavement. Miss Dunsmore said she wasn't offering this as consolation but apparently elephants go into mourning and so, very strangely, does the pike. So we chatted about that for a bit. Told me not to take any big decisions, and if I was throwing away any of his books could I steer them her way as she ran some sort of reading service for the disabled.

I dropped into the Health Centre and the receptionist said there was a pamphlet on death; they'd had some on the counter, only the tots kept taking them to scribble on, so they hadn't re-ordered. She said she'd skimmed through it and the gist of it was not to take any big decisions and to throw yourself into something. I said, 'You don't mean the canal?' She said, 'Come again?' Nobody expects you to make jokes. As I was going out she called me back and said did Ralph wear spectacles? Because if he did, not to throw away the old pairs as owing to cutbacks they'd started a spectacles recycling scheme.

Back at base Mabel said Margaret had been plonked on the chair in the passage all morning with her bag packed and her outside coat on, and for some reason wellington boots. Said the police were coming. We manhandled her upstairs, and after about seventeen goes I managed to smuggle in a tablet which did the trick and she'd just settled down for a little zizz when who should draw up at the door but Giles.

He'd cancelled all his appointments, eluded the guards at the office and just belted down the A12 because he suddenly thought I might need cheering up, bless him. He could always get round Mabel ever since he was little, so she agrees to hold the fort while he whisks me off to lunch at somewhere rather swish. I thought to myself, I hope you're watching, Ralph, you old rascal, and eating your words. Ralph and Giles never got on for more than five minutes whereas, it's funny, he was always dotty about Mags.

When eventually we get back, what with all the wine etc. (I mean pudding *and* cheese), I'm just longing to put my head down, but Giles cracks the whip and gets me to sign lots of papers. It turns out Ralph's left me very nicely off. What with the house and all his various holdings, one way and another I'm quite a rich lady. He's tied a bit up for Margaret, nothing specific for Giles, but he doesn't mind because of course he doesn't need any and when I go he'll get it all anyway. But what I do have is what Giles calls a liquidity problem, and the first item on the agenda is to give me some ready cash, hence the papers. Then something about buying a forest. Bit wary to start with, said, 'Can I not mull it?' and Giles said, 'Well you can, but the index is going down.' I said, 'What about Mr Sherlock?' Giles said, 'You know what lawyers are.' Wish old Ralph could have seen me, signing away. He never showed me any papers at all, whereas Giles took me through them and explained it all. I suppose it's a different generation. What he did do, which made me feel a tiny bit shifty, was to take away three or four of the best pictures, the two carriage clocks and a couple of other choice items. Said that when the sharks from the revenue came round to assess the stuff for estate duty these were just the

items that would bump the figure up. I said, 'What about the inventory?'
Giles said, 'I think we'll just drag our brogues on that one.' Apparently
everybody does it. He's just going to keep the stuff under the bed at Sloane
Street until the heat is off, then back they come.

Margaret still lying on the bed when I went upstairs. Asleep she looks
quite presentable. Daddy's little girl. Not so little now, those great legs.
But as Mabel says, 'It looks as if we're on the hospital trail again.' If she
goes in, I could perhaps go to Siena. Except I've nobody to go with. One
keeps forgetting that.

Go to black.

Come up on Muriel sitting at a table writing letters. Afternoon.

It's not an ideal place, no one is saying it is. Even Giles doesn't say that. In
fact it's a perfect example of one of those places they're always famously
about to scrap. Started life as a workhouse probably, during the
Napoleonic Wars, and *qua* building not displeasing. As someone weaned
on Nikolaus Pevsner and practically a founder member of the National
Trust I wouldn't alter a single brick. And as an arts centre first rate. As a
museum of industrial archaeology . . . couldn't be bettered. Or as a craft
centre, weaving, pottery, a shop-window where craftsmen and
craftswomen could make and display their wares . . . absolutely ideal, the
very place. But as a mental hospital . . . oh no, no, no, no, no.

The food, for instance. The food has to cross a courtyard – the kitchen is
so far away for all I know it may have to cross a frontier. One toilet per
floor . . . I just put my head round the door and wished I hadn't; no
telephone that I could see and the beds so crammed together if you got out
of one you'd be into another. Dreadful.

And of course I keep thinking of Ridgeways, the cup of tea, the
matron's parlour and that immaculate lawn. It would break old Ralph's
heart. But Ridgeways costs money. It always did. First of the month, beg
to inform, respectfully submit, all very nice but £600 on the dot. And
more. And more. And as Giles says, 'Mummy no can do. That kind of
money we do not have.' Well we do, but it's all tied up.

And whereas in normal circumstances one would have fought tooth and
nail to keep her in the private sector, just out of respect for Daddy,
nowadays we are in what Giles calls a different ball game. And the old
thing minds. Goodness, he minds. I wanted him to come with me today

but just the idea of the place upsets him so much he won't even set foot in
it. And actually I feel the same, but where is that going to get us? I thought
of Ralph (as if I ever think of anybody else) and I thought, 'Come on,
Muriel. You're a widow lady, you've got time on your hands, if anybody's
in a position to roll their sleeves up it's you.' So today when I paid Mags a
visit I got the name of the hospital secretary, almoner it used to be called in
my day, and bearded him in his den. He did have a beard actually and
looked pretty sorry for himself besides. It turns out he has to precept for
absolutely everything down to the last toilet roll, and if he does have any
brainwaves about improvements and can sell them to his own management
committee, he's still at the mercy of the regional spending programme.

I asked about a table-tennis table. He said, 'My point exactly.' A
table-tennis table would mean going cap in hand to Ipswich, which he's
not anxious to do since the vegetable steamer's on its last legs. And on the
rare occasions he does have a bit of latitude he finds his hands are tied by
NUPE. Well, the upshot is I'm writing sheaves of letters to everybody I've
ever heard of in an effort to plug the hospital into the coffee-morning
circuit and get a support group started. What I'm saying is that mental
illness is a scourge. It's also a mystery, can occur in the best-regulated
families and nobody knows why. I mean, take us. Why have we been
singled out? Loving parents. Perfectly normal childhood, then this.

When I went in this afternoon, Margaret was weaving a basket, and not
making a bad stab at it really, all things considered. It's lucky I arrived
when I did because she'd just got to the part where she had to integrate the
handle with the main body and she was making a real pig's breakfast of it.
So I got cracking and showed her the whys and wherefores and actually
ended up making both handles. Which seemed to make her a lot happier.
She's never been much good with her hands. Giles was a real wizard.

A propos Giles there's a bit of a crisis with the funds apparently. Nothing
serious. A chum's let him down. Didn't read the small print. Says it's
nothing to worry about, though we may have to pull our horns in a bit
further. So I said, 'All hands to the pumps. With all Daddy's contacts in
the City why don't I start up a little catering business, executive lunches
and the like? Good nursery food and lashings of it.' Giles not sure. Thought
these days they wanted something a bit more nouvelle. I laughed, I said,
'Don't you believe it. Men are overgrown schoolboys, always were.
Preached salad at Ralph for years and what good did it do?' Giles said,
'Small detail, Mum: what are you going to use for capital?' So that put the

tin hat on that one. It's this bloody liquidity thing. It's funny I never heard Ralph mention it.

Go to black.

Come up on Muriel in a bare unfurnished room. A suitcase open. A tea-chest. Afternoon.

Job sorting out the one or two things I want to keep, though quite honestly I'm not sorry to see the back of most of it. I feel it puts me more in the same boat as Ralph. Lay not up for yourself treasures on earth type thing. The lilies of the field syndrome. Said this to the vicar who was looking round. He thought this was a healthy attitude and how much did I think the walnut sidetable might fetch, it would go so well in their hall. Huge marquee on the lawn. People trooping through the house, and Angela Gillespie never away. Said how horrid it must be to see people poking about among one's prized possessions. I said, 'Yes,' but it isn't really. The person I do feel sorry for is Mabel, who's had it to polish all these years.

Still, she was getting on like a house on fire with the auctioneer's men, who were all so careful and polite I'd have married any one of them on the spot. Angela beefing on about all the dealers being here, putting up the prices, I thought good job. Still, however much it all fetches it will only be a drop in the ocean.

At one point Angela got the Duttons in a corner and started telling the tale. Said Giles had always been a wrong 'un. I turned round and said she didn't know what she was talking about, it had been a genuine mistake. She said, 'Mistake? Hundreds of people losing their life savings a mistake?' I said, 'So why do you think I'm selling up?' She said, 'It wasn't your fault. Why should you suffer? That's what worries me, Muriel, it's not fair on you.' Fair on me or not it didn't stop her buying the corner cupboard. She's had her eye on it for years.

I suppose Giles has been a scamp. But I don't think he's been wicked. Just not very bright that's all. Still, Sloane Street is in Pippa's name so that's a blessing, and the school fees were covenanted for years ago so it's not all gloom. I sat under the chestnut tree while the sale was going on, and thought how none of this would have happened if Ralph hadn't died. Then I heard him say, 'Buck up, old girl,' and went and gave a hand with the tea. I haven't told Margaret yet. Her fourteen-year-old psychiatrist thinks this may not be the moment. Sees some signs of improvement. Margaret brought him some tulips last week. Picked them from one of the hospital flowerbeds. I apologised and said I could give them some of our bulbs. He said not at all, it was a sign she was becoming more outgoing. Wanted to know about Ralph and Margaret. I said, 'In what way?' He said, 'No particular way. When she was little.' I said, 'Ralph was fond of her: she was his little girl.' He said, 'Yes.'

Took the dogs up the hill later on. They're next I suppose. Bloody psychiatrist.

Go to black.

Come up on Muriel in a plain boarding-house room. Evening.

Crack of dawn this morning I routed out my trusty green cossy and spent a happy half-hour breasting the billows. The old cossy's seen better days and the moth has got into the bust but as the only people about were one or two brave souls walking the dog I didn't frighten the troops.

Came back hungry as a hunter so boiled myself an egg on the ring and had it with a slice of Ryvita, sitting in the window. Sun just catches it for an hour then, lovely. I tidied the room, did one or two jobs, and then toddled along to the library and had a walk round Boots by which time it was getting on for lunchtime, it's surprising how time does go. When I think of the things I used to get through in the old days I wonder how I did it.

Been here about a month now. Got onto it via an advert in *The Lady*. Sledmere it's called, 'Holiday flatlets'. Off season, of course, and quite reasonable. I haven't quite got the town sorted out yet. I feel sure there must be a community here if only I can put my finger on it. I had a word with a young woman at the Town Hall. Blue fingernails but civil enough otherwise. Said was I interested in Meals On Wheels. I said, 'Rather. I was 2 i/c Meals on Wheels for the whole of Sudbury,' a fund of experience. Brawn not too good but brains available to be picked at any time. She looked a bit blank. Turns out she meant did I want to be on the receiving end. I said, 'Not on your life.' But message received and understood. The old girl's past it. Hence the swim, I suppose.

Still, I soldier on and it's not quite orphans of the storm time. I look round the shops quite a bit and if I'm lucky I run into Angela Gillespie who's got her mother in a home here and comes over from time to time. We have coffee and a natter about the old days. Though I can't do that too often. Morning coffee these days seems to cost a king's ransom. And with me there doesn't have to be coffee. I can talk to anybody. The other morning I got chatting to one of these young men in orange who bang their tambourines in the precinct. Came up to me rattling his bowl, shaven head but otherwise quite sensible. His view is that life is some kind of prep. Trial run. Thinks we're being buffed up for a better role next time. As sensible as anything else I suppose. I said, 'Well, I just hope it's not in Hunstanton.' (*She laughs*).

The big bright spot on the horizon is Margaret. Heaps better, lost a lot of weight, got rid of that terrible cardigan and now is quite a good-looking young woman. In a hostel up to pres. but planning on getting a small flat. Came down last week and says next time it could be under her own steam, takes her driving test in ten days. Miracle. She took me out to lunch just like a normal girl. Talked about Ralph etc. Doesn't blame him, wishes he were alive. I don't know what I think. Sorry for him, I suppose. She paid the bill and left a tip, just as if she'd been doing it all her life. Of course she'll be nicely off now, Ralph tied it all up so tight even Giles couldn't get his hands on it, the rascal.

Don't see him and Pippa much, not a peep out of them for over a month now. Doesn't like to come down, says it upsets him. Don't know why. Doesn't upset me. Miss the tinies. Not so tiny, Lucy'll be twelve now. And twelve is like fifteen. Married next. I'd seen myself as a model grandmother, taking them to Peter Pan and the Science Museum. Not to be. Another dream bites the dust.

My big passion now is the telly box. Never bothered with it before. These days I watch it all the time. And I'm not the discerning viewer. No fear. Rubbish. Australian series in the afternoons, everything. Glued to it all. Fan.

The dialogue is more broken up now.

I sometimes wonder if I killed Ralph. All those death-dealing breakfasts. We haven't had much weather to speak of. Eat less now. A buttered scone goes a long way.

She picks up a Walkman and headphones.

This is my new toy. Seen children with them, never appreciated what they were. Asked a young man for a listen in the precinct. Revelation. Saved up and bought one. Get the cassettes out of the library. Worth its weight in gold. Marvellous.

She puts it on and henceforth speaks in bursts and too loudly.

I wouldn't want you to think this was a tragic story.

Pause.

I'm not a tragic woman.

Pause.

I'm not that type.

Fade out to the faint sound of the music, possibly Johann Strauss.

A Cream Cracker Under the Settee

DORIS   Thora Hird
POLICEMAN   Steven Beard

Produced by Innes Lloyd
Directed by Stuart Burge
Designed by Tony Burrough
Music by George Fenton

Doris is in her seventies and the play is set in the living-room and hallway of her semi-detached house. She is sitting slightly awkwardly on a low chair and rubbing her leg. Morning.

It's such a silly thing to have done.

   Pause.

I should never have tried to dust. Zulema says to me every time she comes, 'Doris. Do not attempt to dust. The dusting is my department. That's what the council pay me for. You are now a lady of leisure. Your dusting days are over.' Which would be all right provided she did dust. But Zulema doesn't dust. She half-dusts. I know when a place isn't clean.

   When she's going she says, 'Doris. I don't want to hear that you've been touching the Ewbank. The Ewbank is out of bounds.' I said, 'I could just run round with it now and again.' She said, 'You can't run anywhere. You're on trial here.' I said, 'What for?' She said, 'For being on your own. For not behaving sensibly. For not acting like a woman of seventy-five who has a pacemaker and dizzy spells and doesn't have the sense she was born with.' I said, 'Yes, Zulema.'

   She says, 'What you don't understand, Doris, is that I am the only person that stands between you and Stafford House. I have to report on you. The Welfare say to me every time, "Well, Zulema, how is she coping? Wouldn't she be better off in Stafford House?"' I said, 'They don't put people in Stafford House just for running round with the Ewbank.' 'No,' she says. 'They bend over backwards to keep you in your own home. But, Doris, you've got to meet them half-way. You're seventy-five. Pull your horns in. You don't have to swill the flags. You don't have to clean the bath. Let the dirt wait. It won't kill you. I'm here every week.'

   I was glad when she'd gone, dictating. I sat for a bit looking up at me and Wilfred on the wedding photo. And I thought, 'Well, Zulema, I bet you haven't dusted the top of that.' I used to be able to reach only I can't now. So I got the buffet and climbed up. And she hadn't. Thick with dust. Home help. Home hindrance. You're better off doing it yourself. And I was just wiping it over when, oh hell, the flaming buffet went over.

   Pause.

You feel such a fool. I can just hear Zulema. 'Well, Doris, I did tell you.' Only I think I'm all right. My leg's a bit numb but I've managed to get back on the chair. I'm just going to sit and come round a bit. Shakes you up, a fall.

Pause.

Shan't let on I was dusting.

She shoves the duster down the side of the chair.

Dusting is forbidden.

She looks down at the wedding photo on the floor.

Cracked the photo. We're cracked, Wilfred.

Pause.

The gate's open again. I thought it had blown shut, only now it's blown open. Bang bang bang all morning, it'll be bang bang bang all afternoon.

Dogs coming in, all sorts. You see Zulema should have closed that, only she didn't.

Pause.

The sneck's loose, that's the root cause of it. It's wanted doing for years. I kept saying to Wilfred, 'When are you going to get round to that gate?' But oh no. It was always the same refrain. 'Don't worry, Mother. I've got it on my list.' I never saw no list. He had no list. I was the one with the list. He'd no system at all, Wilfred. 'When I get a minute, Doris.' Well, he's got a minute now, bless him.

Pause.

Feels funny this leg. Not there.

Pause.

Some leaves coming down now. I could do with trees if they didn't have leaves, going up and down the path. Zulema won't touch them. Says if I want leaves swept I've to contact the Parks Department.

I wouldn't care if they were my leaves. They're not my leaves. They're next-door's leaves. We don't have any leaves. I know that for a fact. We've only got the one little bush and it's an evergreen, so I'm certain they're not my leaves. Only other folks won't know that. They see the bush and they see the path and they think, 'Them's her leaves.' Well, they're not.

I ought to put a note on the gate. 'Not my leaves.' Not my leg either, the way it feels. Gone to sleep.

Pause.

I didn't even want the bush, to be quite honest. We debated it for long enough. I said, 'Dad. Is it a bush that will make a mess?' He said, 'Doris. Rest assured. This type of bush is very easy to follow,' and fetches out the catalogue. ' "This labour-saving variety is much favoured by retired people." Anyway,' he says, 'the garden is my department.' Garden! It's only the size of a tablecloth. I said, 'Given a choice, Wilfred, I'd have preferred concrete.' He said, 'Doris. Concrete has no character.' I said, 'Never mind character, Wilfred, where does hygiene come on the agenda?' With concrete you can feel easy in your mind. But no. He had to have his little garden even if it was only a bush. Well, he's got his little garden now. Only I bet that's covered in leaves. Graves, gardens, everything's to follow.

I'll make a move in a minute. See if I can't put the kettle on. Come on leg. Wake up.

Go to black.

Come up on Doris sitting on the floor with her back to the wall. The edge of a tiled fireplace also in shot.

Fancy, there's a cream cracker under the settee. How long has that been there? I can't think when I last had cream crackers. She's not half done this place, Zulema.

I'm going to save that cream cracker and show it her next time she starts going on about Stafford House. I'll say, 'Don't Stafford House me, lady. This cream cracker was under the settee. I've only got to send this cream cracker to the Director of Social Services and you'll be on the carpet. Same as the cream cracker. I'll be in Stafford House, Zulema, but you'll be in the Unemployment Exchange.'

I'm en route for the window only I'm not making much headway. I'll bang on it. Alert somebody. Don't know who. Don't know anybody round here now. Folks opposite, I don't know them. Used to be the Marsdens. Mr and Mrs Marsden and Yvonne, the funny daughter. There for years. Here before we were, the Marsdens. Then he died, and she died, and Yvonne went away somewhere. A home, I expect.

Smartish woman after them. Worked at Wheatley and Whiteley, had a three-quarter-length coat. Used to fetch the envelopes round for the blind. Then she went and folks started to come and go. You lose track. I don't think they're married, half of them. You see all sorts. They come in the garden and behave like animals. I find the evidence in a morning.

She picks up the photograph that has fallen from the wall.

Now, Wilfred.

Pause.

I can nip this leg and nothing.

Pause.

Ought to have had a dog. Then it could have been barking of someone. Wilfred was always hankering after a dog. I wasn't keen. Hairs all up and down, then having to take it outside every five minutes. Wilfred said he would be prepared to undertake that responsibility. The dog would be his province. I said, 'Yes, and whose province would all the little hairs be?' I gave in in the finish, only I said it had to be on the small side. I didn't want one of them great lolloping, lamp post-smelling articles. And we never got one either. It was the growing mushrooms in the cellar saga all over again. He never got round to it. A kiddy'd've solved all that. Getting mad ideas. Like the fretwork, making toys and forts and whatnot. No end of money he was going to make. Then there was his phantom allotment. Oh, he was going to be coming home with leeks and spring cabbage and I don't know what. 'We can be self-sufficient in the vegetable department, Doris.' Never materialised. I was glad. It'd've meant muck somehow.

Hello. Somebody coming. Salvation.

She cranes up towards the window.

Young lad. Hello. Hello.

She begins to wave.

The cheeky monkey. He's spending a penny. Hey.

She shouts.

Hey. Get out. Go on. Clear off. You little demon. Would you credit it? Inside our gate. Broad daylight. The place'll stink.

A pause as she realises what she has done.

He wouldn't have known what to do anyway. Only a kiddy. The policeman comes past now and again. If I can catch him. Maybe the door's a better bet. If I can get there I can open it and wait while somebody comes past.

She starts to heave herself up.

This must be what they give them them frame things for.

Go to black.

Come up on Doris sitting on the floor in the hall, her back against the front door, the letter-box above her head.

This is where we had the pram. You couldn't get past for it. Proper prams then, springs and hoods. Big wheels. More like cars than prams. Not these fold-up jobs. You were proud of your pram. Wilfred spotted it in the *Evening Post.* I said, 'Don't let's jump the gun, Wilfred.' He said, 'At that price, Doris? This is the chance of a lifetime.'

Pause.

Comes under this door like a knife. I can't reach the lock. That's part of the Zulema regime. 'Lock it and put it on the chain, Doris. You never know who comes. It may not be a bona fide caller.' It never is a bona fide caller. I never get a bona fide caller.

Couple came round last week. Braying on the door. They weren't bona fide callers, they had a Bible. I didn't go. Only they opened the letter-box and started shouting about Jesus. 'Good news,' they kept shouting. 'Good news.' They left the gate open, never mind good news. They ought to get their priorities right. They want learning that on their instruction course. Shouting about Jesus and leaving gates open. It's hypocrisy is that. It is in my book anyway. 'Love God and close all gates.'

She closes her eyes. We hear some swift steps up the path and the letter-box opens as a leaflet comes through. Swift steps away again as she opens her eyes.

Hello, hello.

She bangs on the door behind her.

Help. Help. Oh stink.

She tries to reach the leaflet.

What is it? Minicabs? 'Your roof repaired'?

She gets the leaflet.

'Grand carpet sale.' Carpet sales in chapels now. Else sikhs.

She looks at the place where the pram was.

I wanted him called John. The midwife said he wasn't fit to be called anything and had we any newspaper? Wilfred said, 'Oh yes. She saves newspaper. She saves shoeboxes as well.' I must have fallen asleep because when I woke up she'd gone. I wanted to see to him. Wrapping him in newspaper as if he was dirty. He wasn't dirty, little thing. I don't think Wilfred minded. A kiddy. It was the same as the allotment and the fretwork. Just a craze. He said, 'We're better off, Doris. Just the two of us.' It was then he started talking about getting a dog.

If it had lived I might have had grandchildren now. Wouldn't have been in this fix. Daughters are best. They don't migrate.

Pause.

I'm going to have to migrate or I'll catch my death.

She nips her other leg.

This one's going numb now.

She picks up the photo.

Come on, Dad. Come on, numby leg.

Go to black.

Come up on Doris sitting with her back against the settee under which she spotted the cream cracker. It is getting dark.

I've had this frock for years. A lame woman ran it up for me that lived down Tong Road. She made me a little jersey costume I used to wear with my tan court shoes. I think I've still got it somewhere. Upstairs. Put away. I've got umpteen pillowcases, some we got given when we were first married. Never used. And the blanket I knitted for the cot. All its little coats and hats.

She puts her hand down.

Here's this cream cracker.

She rubs it.

Naught wrong with it.

She eats it.

Making a lot of crumbs. Have to have a surreptitious go with the Ewbank. 'Doris. The Ewbank is out of bounds.' Out of bounds to her too, by the looks of it. A cream cracker under the settee. She wants reporting. Can't report her now. I've destroyed the evidence.

Pause.

I could put another one under, they'd never know. Except they might say it was me. 'Squatting biscuits under the settee, Doris. You're not fit to be on your own. You'd be better off in Stafford House.'

Pause.

We were always on our own, me and Wilfred. We weren't gregarious. We just weren't the gregarious type. He thought he was, but he wasn't.

Mix. I don't want to mix. Comes to the finish and they suddenly think you want to mix. I don't want to be stuck with a lot of old lasses. And they all smell of pee. And daft half of them, banging tambourines. You go daft there, there's nowhere else for you to go but daft. Wearing somebody else's frock. They even mix up your teeth. I am H.A.P.P.Y. I am not H.A.P.P.Y. I am un-H.A.P.P.Y. Or I would be.

And Zulema says, 'You don't understand, Doris. You're not up to date. They have lockers, now. Flowerbeds. They have their hair done. They go on trips to Wharfedale.' I said, 'Yes. Smelling of pee.' She said, 'You're prejudiced, you.' I said, 'I am, where hygiene's concerned.'

When people were clean and the streets were clean and it was all clean and you could walk down the street and folks smiled and passed the time of day, I'd leave the door on the latch and go on to the end for some toffee, and when I came back Dad was home and the cloth was on and the plates out and we'd have our tea. Then we'd side the pots and I'd wash up while he read the paper and we'd eat the toffees and listen to the wireless all them years ago when we were first married and I was having the baby.

Doris and Wilfred. They don't get called Doris now. They don't get called Wilfred. Museum, names like that. That's what they're all called in Stafford House. Alice and Doris. Mabel and Gladys. Antiques. Keep them under lock and key. 'What's your name? Doris? Right. Pack your case. You belong in Stafford House.'

A home. Not me. No fear.

She closes her eyes. A pause.

POLICEMAN'S VOICE. Hello. Hello.

Doris opens her eyes but doesn't speak.

Are you all right?

Pause.

DORIS. No. I'm all right.
POLICEMAN. Are you sure?
DORIS. Yes.
POLICEMAN. Your light was off.
DORIS. I was having a nap.
POLICEMAN. Sorry. Take care.

He goes.

DORIS. Thank you.

She calls again.

Thank you.

Long pause.

You've done it now, Doris. Done it now, Wilfred.

Pause.

I wish I was ready for bed. All washed and in a clean nightie and the bottle in, all sweet and crisp and clean like when I was little on Baking Night, sat in front of the fire with my long hair still.

Her eyes close and she sings a little to herself. The song, which she only half remembers, is My Alice Blue Gown.

Pause.

Never mind. It's done with now, anyway.

Light fades.